GW01045872

STOATS & WEASELS
POLECATS & MARTENS

STOATS & WEASELS POLECATS & MARTENS

•PADDY SLEEMAN•

with illustrations by
GUY TROUGHTON

Whittet Books

Title page illustration *Stoat on drystone wall.*

First published 1989
Text © 1989 by Paddy Sleeman
Illustrations © 1989 by Guy Troughton
Whittet Books Ltd, 18 Anley Road, London W14 0BY

Design by Richard Kelly

British Library Cataloguing in Publication Data

Sleeman, Paddy
    Stoats and weasels: polecats and martens.
    1. Mustelidae
    I. Title
    599.74'447

ISBN 0–905483–75–8

Typeset by Litho Link Limited, Welshpool.

Printed and bound by Biddles of Guildford.

Contents

Acknowledgments 7

Preface 9

Introduction 11

Weasels 14

Stoats 20

Coat colour in weasels and stoats 27

Polecats 31

Martens 35

Habitats 41

Relations with each other 44

Relations with man 48

Ecological roles 53

Breeding 55

Growing up 59

Dispersing 64

Denning 67

Food 71

Predators 76

Parasites 80

Signs 83

Smells 89

Scientific studies 91

Energetics 96

Captive and tame small mustelids 98

Folklore 101

Conservation 103

Useful addresses   *109*

References   *111*

Index   *115*

Acknowledgments

I would like to thank Johnny Brown and Pat Fox, an Irishman and an Englishman, both of whom took time to teach me about wild animals. Pat Fox once showed me a dancing stoat in Hampshire. Johnny Brown often talked to me about weasels (in fact stoats) and how to trap them. This book is based on the work of many scientists, too numerous to mention; I thank them all. However, some scientists have been especially supportive and deserve special mention, in particular Carolyn King in New Zealand, Rodger Powell in the United States, Stephen Tapper in England, Sam Erlinge in Sweden, Sylvain Debrot in Switzerland and Paddy O'Sullivan, Patrick Warner and Martin Speight of the Irish Wildlife Service. I would also like to thank some of the staff of the British Museum (Natural History) including Ann Baker, Daphne Hills, Sue Angle and Gordon Corbet for help in various ways. Also Michael McInerney, Maire Mulcahy and Tom Cross of the Zoology Department, University College, Cork, provided help, encouragement and ideas. My family, Carolyn and the inmates of 5, Carrigduhn for understanding. Finally, I am very grateful to Annabel Whittet for constant encouragement and textual improvements and Irene O'Sullivan who typed this at very short notice.

Preface

To many people the animals dealt with in this book are either vermin or fur-bearers: the former to be persecuted because they might kill poultry and game birds, the latter to be killed for their fur. However, such attitudes are rapidly changing and informed people now regard these small predators in a very different light. They are interested in the animals for their own sake, and not for what they can or cannot do for man. It is to satisfy such interests that this book was written.

I have attempted to present factual, scientific information about these animals, but at the same time I have tried to avoid getting too serious, scientific and boring. To understand ecology it is important to focus on populations of such animals, as well as individuals; also to show how they relate to other animals and animal communities. I have attempted to describe small populations of each species in areas where they have been studied: weasels in Oxfordshire; stoats in County Cork; polecats in Mid Wales and martens in County Clare. It is hoped that these descriptions will give some insight into the actual species in its natural state and how research is done. However, comparatively little research has been done on the animals that are the subject of this book, so there are large gaps in our knowledge, which I shall point out.

My own interest did not start with science. As a boy wandering around the Irish countryside, I would occasionally come across the Irish stoats, always called weasels in Ireland. The stoat's sleek, bendable body and lack of fear prompted both my admiration and fascination. Later, as a student in Ulster, while studying territoriality in robins in a wood, I had the pleasure of seeing an Irish stoat, followed by another. For the next twenty minutes or so I had the unexpected delight of watching one of nature's most lithe creatures at work. From then on I was hooked. As a graduate I worked on martens, studying their ectoparasites — fleas, ticks and mites. Then, after a few years studying deer and their parasites, I spent five years studying the Irish stoat. Many people helped by sending me dead stoats — mainly road casualties — from all over Ireland. By the end of each day spent examining them I often smelt rather like a stoat myself! At the time I also studied live wild stoats on Fota Estate, near Cork City.

These studies taught me something about weasels, stoats, polecats and martens; I hope I have put across some useful information in this book. And anyway, God forgive me, I've enjoyed every minute of it.

January 1989   *Paddy Sleeman*

9

Introduction

Animals basically eat two types of food: plants or other animals. Those animals that eat plants (called herbivores) do not normally have any trouble finding their food. Plants do not run away, although they may be difficult to digest, which requires complex adaptations by the animals that eat them.

Animals that eat other animals (called carnivores) have little trouble dealing with their food. By comparison with plants, animal flesh is easily digested and highly nutritious. The difficulty in being a carnivore is that prey, other animals, will not sit still and wait to be eaten. Rather they will run away and hide. For this reason and because the carnivore's role is highly competitive, such animals have tended to become specialized.

The animals that are the subjects of this book are such specialized carnivores. They are all members of the weasel family called the mustelidae. This family includes other specialized carnivores, for example otters, which specialize in feeding on fish; and badgers, which, in Europe, specialize in feeding on earthworms. The species dealt with here, weasels, stoats, martens and polecats, are the smaller members of the mustelidae and are referred to hereafter as the small mustelids.

The members of the weasel family we are interested in belong to two groups: the genus mustela and the genus martes (see diagram on p. 13). The weasel, stoat and polecat are all in genus mustela. So are ferrets,

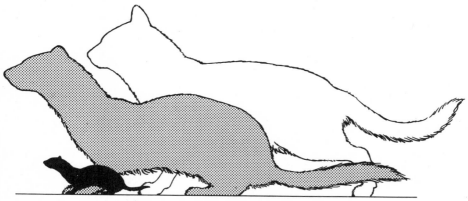

Relative sizes of weasel, pine marten and cat.

which are domesticated polecats, and mink, which were introduced to this country by fur farmers this century. It has long been thought that weasels and stoats are very closely related. However, as we shall see later, this may not be true. The martens are in a separate genus, martes (along with sables). The reasoning for this may not be correct and it is possible that they are more closely related to stoats than weasels (see Breeding).

The book mainly deals with British small mustelids, but also draws on examples from elsewhere in Europe, North America and other parts of the world. For example, some small mustelids have been successfully introduced to New Zealand and I will talk about these later.

Small mustelids, like all the weasel family, have obvious anal scent glands which produce pungent gooey liquids. The animals are long and thin, with short legs, and vary greatly in size from 500 mm (20 inches) long (head and body length of martens) to 165 mm (6½ inches) long (weasels). Size is so variable between sexes and from place to place, that they are presented here by ranges of size (see diagram). Essentially the weasel is the smallest and the marten the biggest, but there are huge overlaps in size and weight between the species. Their bone structure illustrates their long, thin shape (see drawing), which is important in allowing them access to some prey habitats. Their skulls (see drawing) have long flattened craniums and they have two prominent pointed teeth called canines.

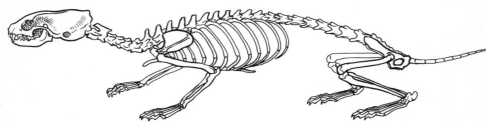

Weasel skeleton.

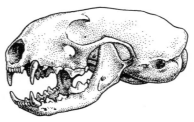

Stoat skull.

Because they are carnivores, they are naturally rare. Think of a weasel in an English wood. The weasel needs roughly 25 grams (.8 oz) of food per day, which is the equivalent of one or more small mammals, in this case mainly wood mice and bank voles.Therefore, per day, just to survive, the weasel will need to kill one small mammal all year round. Now think of the needs of the weasel's mate, its family and other predators and you will realize why there must be enormous numbers of such small mammals per weasel. Hence in our English wood, mice and voles are common; weasels, by comparison, are rare.

As stoats, polecats and martens are bigger, they need more prey and are therefore even less common. As we shall see later the presence and number of prey available to these animals determines much of their lives. At best the weasels, stoats, polecats and martens are sparsely distributed; if there are insufficient prey animals around, they are not present at all. Do not therefore expect to see them often, and when you do see them remember you have been most fortunate.

The Weasel Family
(There are other members of the family which have been omitted)

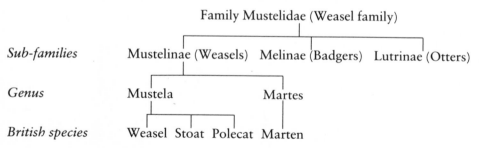

Range of size (head and body) and weight of British small mustelids

	Head & body (mm)	Weight (g)
Weasel	170-230	35-202
Stoat	240-310	140-445
Polecat	290-460	442-1522
Marten	430-507	1049-1418

Weasels

Weasels are the smallest of the small mustelids (see diagram); indeed they are the smallest carnivores on earth. The ones in Britain are not the very smallest, which are found in North America and are called 'least weasels': an example of something American being smaller rather than bigger than something here! A small carnivore is something of a surprise, since by definition a carnivore must overpower and kills its prey; to do this, you would expect it to be bigger. However, being small is an advantage because they specialize in hunting small mammals, mainly voles, mice and such like, in their burrows and runways. They can fit into such places easily. So small are weasels' heads that there is an old country saying that a weasel's skull will fit through a hole the size of a wedding ring. Given a small weasel and a big ring, this is true.

Weasels are active both by day and night. They may use daylight as an attempt to avoid predation by owls in certain habitats. They have been reported feeding on prey of very different sizes, ranging from worms to

Weasel above ground.

Weasel in characteristic pose.

rats and rabbits. They have also been seen trying to kill young crows and squirrels. They appear to attack such larger prey when they are in a family group (see Growing up). Due to their small size, weasels are vulnerable to cold and larger predators. They can, and do, die from cold, particularly if confined in a cold damp trap without bedding. They also can be, and are, killed by bigger predators, both larger mammal predators, which tend not to eat them because they taste nasty, and large birds of prey, which will eat them because birds cannot smell.

However, their small size also means that they can live on less than the larger members of the weasel family; as we have seen, this makes them more common, and more frequently seen. A characteristic pose for a weasel is standing on its hind legs investigating its surroundings (see drawing). People often do not know if they have seen a weasel or a stoat. What is the difference?

Firstly, stoats are bigger, but size is a unreliable guide to animal identification because individual animals vary considerably in size and because size is very difficult to judge in the usual fleeting glimpse of a wild animal. Stoats have a longer tail and it ends in a black tip. So if you see a black tip to the tail you can definitely say it is a stoat.

In Britain and most of western Europe, weasels do not go white in winter and have an irregular line between the russet-brown back and white belly (see Coat colour). This irregular pattern is different for each weasel, so when studying wild weasels this can be used as a method of identifying individuals. Stoats quite often go white in winter and have a regular line between the back and belly. That is another good guide to identification. But, just to complicate matters, the stoats that occur in Ireland, the Isle of Man and some Scottish offshore islands have irregular back/belly lines like the weasel (see Stoats).

Weasels occur throughout most of Europe (except Ireland), most of Asia, parts of North Africa and a great deal of North America. They are not good island colonizers and are, therefore, not found on many offshore islands. They were introduced to New Zealand, but have never established large populations there. However, they are prolific breeders, often having two litters a year. They can be regarded as one of the most successful and widespread carnivores in the world.

One final word here about weasels is the name itself. In Britain, weasels are called weasels and stoats are called stoats. In Ireland, probably because the Irish stoat is different and because of the way English came to be

Weasel hunting on stone wall.

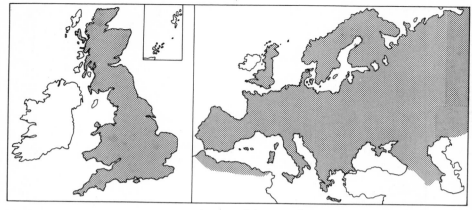

Distribution of the weasel.

spoken in Ireland, stoats are always called weasels. In North America all smaller mustelids are called weasels. So they have a 'least weasel', which is the small weasel already mentioned, a 'short-tail weasel' which is the equivalent of our stoat and a 'long-tail weasel' which is a larger animal unique to North America. Confusing, is it not?

The weasels of Wytham Wood

Wytham Wood is a mainly mature deciduous woodland a few miles west of the city of Oxford. For many years scientists from Oxford University have studied the animals in the wood and now it is probably the best known animal community anywhere in the world. Quite a lot is known about the weasels of Wytham. They live solitary lives, except when breeding, they are often active by day and survive on average for less than a year. The males have territories (defended areas) of 7-15 hectares (17-37 acres), the females have smaller territories of 1-4 hectares (2-9 acres), usually within the territory of a male. They feed mainly on bank voles, but also on field voles, woodmice, rabbits and even occasionally moles. They do not have a significant impact on the populations of voles and mice and they avoid shrews which are common in the wood. They also take large numbers of birds and their eggs in the spring. They even raid bird nest-boxes put out by Oxford scientists. One weasel was photographed departing from a nest-box entrance with a nestling tit. It has been established that the weasels have a significant impact on the tit populations, unlike the rodents, and take more birds when voles are scarce. On the other hand, weasels also regularly turn up as prey of the wood's tawny owls, so there is give and take between the wood's birds and weasels. It is likely that Wytham's weasels are principally active by day to try to avoid the night-flying owls. Unfortunately, stoats are rare at Wytham and martens and polecats have long gone from this part of England. Not many studies of these species have been conducted; it is a shame they didn't also live in Wytham Wood.

Stoats

The stoat is usually bigger than the weasel. However, this is an unreliable way to tell the difference. The characteristic black-tipped tail of the stoat is what you ought to look for. As stoats are bigger they are more often above ground than weasels and as a result they put themselves at risk from attack by birds of prey.

Stoat above ground.

A stoat bearing down on a rabbit.

This is where the black-tipped tail comes in. If a stoat is caught in the open by a bird of prey, as the bird attacks the stoat will whisk its tail up at the last moment, to distract the bird's attention and, more importantly, the attention of the bird's talons. Quite a strategy — which appears to work. I found that among male Irish stoats, the tails often got shorter as they got older, which may be the result of losing parts of their tails in such encounters with birds of prey; surviving with a slightly shorter tail is obviously preferable to not surviving at all.

As they are bigger than weasels, stoats prey on bigger animals, namely rabbits, water voles (where they occur) and birds. They probably

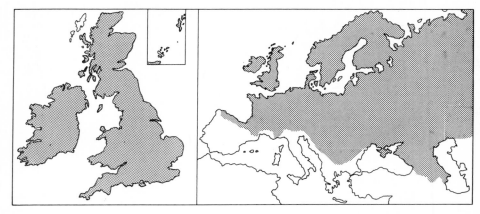

Distribution of the stoat.

originally specialized in feeding on water voles and still feed mainly on such voles in much of Europe. Such voles were once much more plentiful in Britain and occurred away from water, as they still do in much of Europe. However, in Britain and elsewhere, where water voles are scarce or absent, rabbits are now the major prey of stoats. Stoats have a much more flexible diet than weasels, eating a variety of prey, and will adapt to habitats where small mammal prey is relatively scarce.

The interaction between stoats and rabbits is one of the most often discussed aspects of stoats' lives. When hunting, stoats appear to choose one particular rabbit out of several and follow that individual relentlessly until the kill. Sometimes the victim rabbit will give up and freeze, squealing and waiting for its end. It is probable that rabbits in such a situation sometimes die of fright, without physical injury. It is the ability to frighten to death an animal much bigger than itself that has attracted attention. An adult rabbit can weight around 1,200-2,000 g (2 lb 10 oz-4 lb 6 oz), whereas a stoat will weigh a maximum of 445 g (approx 1 lb). Quite remarkable.

People sometimes become involved when they hear the rabbit's squeals and often, quite naturally, deny the stoat its meal by rescuing the rabbit. Seeing such a stricken animal makes a major impact on people, which they remember and talk about. But what about the stoat? Should one remove a source of food from a wild predator like this? People often forget that the stoat has to eat, and that this hunt of a rabbit has expended a lot of its valuable energy.

Stoats are active during both day and night. They swim and climb well. They will often show little fear of man and will, once seen, disappear, only to reappear moments later to get a clear view of you. So it is worth waiting around for a few moments should you see a stoat. Some people are disturbed by this lack of fear and become frightened or indignant, which is a pity, as the stoat has no malice and is simply checking out another odd creature on its patch. Unfortunately many humans assume that all wild animals should be frightened of them. Stoats are reported to 'dance' or 'charm' prey such as birds and rabbits. The stoat leaps up and down, chases its tail and quite literally dances. This elicits the prey's curiosity. Once the prey is off its guard the stoat gets close enough to kill. I have seen this happen myself — it's very cunning.

Stoats are widely distributed across Europe, Asia and North America. They do not occur in Africa, but were successfully introduced into New Zealand where they have been accused of causing the decline in native birds (see Conservation). Their coat turns white in winter throughout

A stoat using the wrap-around technique to catch a wood mouse (see p.61).

most of the north of their range with only the black tail tip remaining. In this condition, they are known as 'ermine', their other name, and their fur in this condition is highly sought after (see Relations with man). In summer the upper part of a stoat's coat is a russet-brown colour, not unlike that of the weasel. In areas where they do not go white in winter the winter coat is this same colour. The lower part of the stoat's coat is often yellowish white.

Stoats are better at colonizing difficult areas such as islands than weasels. They tend to be successful on offshore islands where weasels fail, probably due to their more flexible diet and their mode of reproduction (see Breeding). This success at colonizing islands is reflected in their presence in, for example, Ireland and New Zealand.

A stoat raiding a bird's nest.

The stoats of Fota

Fota Estate is in County Cork in the south of Ireland, and it was there that the first radiotracking (see Scientific studies) study of Irish stoats was done in 1985. It is well wooded in the manner of lowland estates but also has a lot of farmland and a well known wildlife park. It is about 316 hectares (780 acres) of which almost 100 hectares (247 acres) are wooded. Six Irish stoats were trapped and four were radiotracked there. Some were found to be infested by rodent fleas and woodmouse, shrew and rabbit hairs were found in their scats (droppings). The radiotracked stoats were principally found in the woods though occasionally they would venture across open ground, usually very quickly. The largest area used by one of the stoats, a female we called Sally, who probably had young, was 22 hectares (53 acres), and the smallest area used was 2 hectares (5 acres), again by a female. Such an area is referred to as an animal's 'home range'. The area used by Sally was much bigger than previous estimates of such areas used by females calculated by trapping in Scotland. The radiotracked stoats were seen raiding birds' nests and also stalking rabbits and hunting rats in a haystack in the wildlife park. They often denned in rat burrows, but also used rabbit and woodmouse burrows. Sally once had a den up in a lime tree about 2 metres (6½ feet) off the ground. The stoats frequently climbed trees and one even climbed into one of the cages in the wildlife park and ate all but one of the parakeets. The wildlife park staff were not amused.

The Irish stoat — a mysterious mustelid

In 1895, scientists found what they considered was an intermediate form between the weasel and the stoat. This was the Irish stoat, found only in Ireland and the Isle of Man. A similar animal is found on the Scottish islands of Islay and Jura. It appeared to be smaller than a British stoat but larger than a weasel. It had a black tip to its tail like a stoat but an irregular back/belly line like a weasel.

Later ecologists studying British stoats and weasels speculated that they were different in size to avoid competing. They live in the same habitats on the same prey, so they would be expected to compete. Ecologists argue that they became different in size (the stoat getting bigger and the weasel smaller) and this affected their behaviour. For example, bigger stoats would eat bigger prey and smaller weasels would eat smaller prey and in this way they would avoid or minimize competition. To 'prove' this they went to a place where there are no weasels (Ireland) and found a smaller stoat, indeed a stoat that appeared to be halfway in size between the British stoat and weasel.

In fact Irish stoats can and do, in some parts of Ireland, get as big as British stoats, so their size is variable, as are the sizes of British stoats and weasels. The irregular back/belly line of the Irish stoat appears to be linked to the fact that they do not go white in winter, not that they are a semi-weasel. Pity that, for it was a good story.

Coat colour in weasels and stoats

British stoat

Irish stoat

Weasel

In Britain, stoats usually turn white in winter in northern Scotland, but not usually in southern England. The turning white of the stoat's fur is controlled by day-length, sex hormones, and temperature. There are many areas in Britain where some stoats turn white, others do not, retaining their summer coat colour, and sometimes animals turn partially white. All

stoats on the British mainland have a straight back/belly line in summer between the brown of the back and the white of the belly.

Irish stoats almost never turn white, there appears to be only a single recorded instance of a truly white Irish stoat. As prolonged snow cover is rare in Ireland this is understandable. Irish stoats have a irregular, wiggly back/belly line all year round. Weasels in Britain do not turn white and have an irregular, wiggly back/belly line, which was one of the reasons for the confusion about the Irish stoat being intermediate between the stoat and weasel (see previous chapter). However, further north in their range, in northern Scandinavia for example, weasels do turn white in winter. These northern weasels that turn white have a straight back/belly line.

There is one other area besides Ireland, the Isle of Man and Islay and Jura, in the range of the stoat where they have irregular back/belly lines. This is in North America, in coastal British Columbia in Canada and in Washington and Oregon states in the United States (see map). Like Ireland, the areas where these stoats occur have little or no snow cover in winter. These facts strongly suggest that straight back/belly lines are found in weasel and stoat populations which can go white in winter and irregular or wiggly back/belly lines are found in populations that do not go white. Presumably stoats in the south of England retain their ability to go white, and therefore have straight back/belly lines, just in case.

The fact that weasels do not turn white, except much further north than the stoat, may be a reflection of the amount of time each species spends above ground, and thus exposed against the snow. It is not known why the regularity of the back/belly line appears linked to winter whitening. It is possible that the two are linked genetically, or it may be that irregular back/belly lines are better camouflage when there is no snow in winter. One thing is certain, however, that such coat colour changes are important to the animals' survival or else they would not occur. The retention of the black tip tail when stoats turn white suggests predation by birds of prey, which is not uncommon for such small mustelids (see Predators), is an important factor in coat colour change. Winter, when ground cover is minimal, is possibly the time of year when they are most at risk from such birds, so it is not surprising that they have such adaptations.

An ermine at the water's edge in winter.

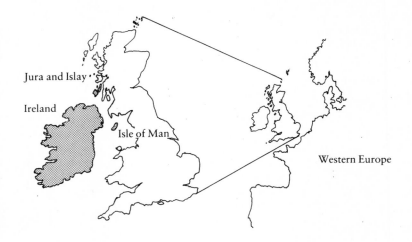

Areas of occurrence

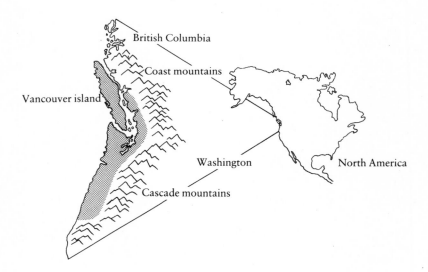

Areas of western Europe and North America where dark stoats with irregular back-belly lines occur.

Polecats

Polecats are bigger than stoats, yet usually smaller than martens (see diagram). Their most characteristic feature is a black stripe across the face, highlighted by white areas on either side (see drawing). This flamboyant marking probably acts as a warning to predators telling them that polecats taste nasty. Certainly they do smell (and therefore probably taste) very nasty. Their noxious smell is mainly produced by their anal scent glands which play a part in defence against would-be predators and territory marking. If excited or frightened, polecats like other small mustelids eject a foul-smelling mixture from these glands which usually persuades would-be predators that they are not worth it. This foul smell is responsible for

Polecat.

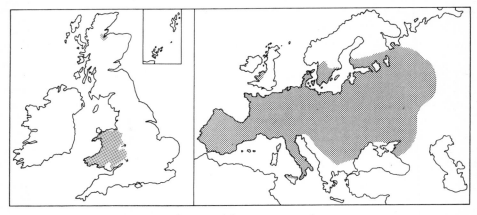

Distribution of the European polecat.

their alternative names: 'foulmart' or 'foulmarten'; the phrase 'to smell like a polecat' needs no explanation. By contrast, martens have the alternative names of 'sweetmarts' or 'sweetmartens'; in my experience they do have a not unpleasant smell.

Polecats' fur is quite distinctive; this and their unique facial pattern distinguishes them from mink, which they otherwise resemble. The polecat's fur is made up of creamy wool mixed with light and dark long guard hairs, with the black guard hairs being most obvious. They have a darkish creamy appearance from a distance. By contrast, mink have dark-brown guard hairs and grey-brown underfur, giving them a sort of chocolate appearance.

Wild polecats are mainly active at night but sometimes in daylight. They amble along, usually searching for prey by sniffing the ground with their bodies held almost level. They are not good climbers and appear to avoid swimming. They will eat almost any mammal they can kill, including rabbits, hares, voles, mice and hedgehogs. They will also eat birds, frogs, lizards and insects.

In Europe and Asia, there are two very similar species of polecat: the European polecat, which is the species that occurs in Britain and Western Europe and the Steppe polecat which is slightly different and occurs on the Steppe of central Europe and Asia. These two species are difficult to tell apart, the Steppe polecat being slightly lighter in colour, but they occur in different habitats and are not found together; you are therefore unlikely to mistake them.

The ferret is a domesticated polecat which has been used by man to bolt both rabbits and rats for at least 2,000 years. It is frequently albino (with characteristic red eyes) or pale coloured, but may have normal polecat coloration. It is not known whether the ferret originated from European or Steppe polecats, but they can and do cross-breed with European polecats, which produces vigorous, fertile offspring. Besides being used by man to hunt rats and rabbits, ferrets are also used in civil engineering to thread wires such as telephone wires through long pipes: they are just the right shape and size for such a job.

Escaped ferrets can be encountered almost anywhere, since they are often lost when working. They are also deliberately released by people in an attempt to control rats and rabbits. It is common practice for pig farmers, for example, to release a ferret or two in rat-infested piggeries. Such animals would not often be recaptured. Such escaped, or deliberately released ferrets sometimes establish feral (wild breeding) populations. Such ferrets exist on many islands including the Isle of Man, Anglesey, Mull, Arran, Bute, the Azores, Sardinia, Sicily and New Zealand. On the island of Harris, off Scotland, they are said to be responsible for exterminating ptarmigan. There are a few feral polecat populations on mainland locations as well, usually in areas where rabbits are plentiful; but they seem more readily to establish themselves on islands. Should you come across a dead polecat/ferret, the only sure way to establish whether it is a true polecat is to measure the post-orbital region of the skull (see drawing). This is usually narrower in ferrets than in polecats: under 16 mm in ferrets, over 16 mm in polecats. The European polecat is reported to be principally a creature of river valleys, less common in mountainous or hilly regions.

Difference between skulls of two species (polecat on left, ferret on right); *note the constriction in front of the cranium between the eyes on the ferret.*

Polecats storing live frogs and toads — fact or fiction?

Like most carnivores, small mustelids store or cache food in times of surplus. Polecats are no exception. A bizarre and somewhat unbelievable story is told of their storing of frogs and toads alive! They are said to bite the amphibians at the base of the skull so that they are paralysed yet not killed. These are said to be stored in underground chambers. By this method the polecat would provide itself with fresh prey in the winter.

Hoards of between 40-120 such paralysed hapless amphibians have been reported. Given the polecat's alleged ferocity and the hatred felt for it by those involved in game preservation, this story has often been quoted as evidence of the animal's obvious cruelty. However, if true, it is only the animal behaving by instinct rather than from malignant intent. It could be true, for moles are known to store earthworms in a similar fashion.

The polecats of Llandrindod Wells

Llandrindod Wells is a small town in the hills of central Wales. It is at the centre of the polecat's current range in Britain and the surrounding area is characteristic of the remote hilly areas in which British polecats survived for the last hundred years or so. It is no accident that it shares this rugged habitat with similarly persecuted birds of prey such as red kites and buzzards. The Ministry of Agriculture has a field station in Llandrindod to study foxes, rabbits and sometimes moles. As polecats are important local predators of rabbits in the area, attempts were made to study them by radiotracking in the 1970s. These studies were dogged by problems such as the polecats losing the radio-tags, radio-tags malfunctioning and the terrain, which makes radio signals difficult to receive accurately. Nevertheless these studies did tell us that the polecats were active at night, sometimes active all night. During the day they would be found underground in dens such as rabbit burrows, badger setts and barns. They were active over large areas, the largest recorded being 150 hectares (370 acres) and they might travel up to 2 kilometres (1.2 miles).

Martens

The name 'marten' is a recent innovation. Originally they were called 'marterns', but then it became 'martin'. This caused confusion with the bird of that name so now marten is used.

The martens are the largest of the small mustelids. The pine marten, the only species found in Britain and Ireland, stands about 15 cm (6 inches) at the shoulder and is usually bigger than the polecat (see diagram on p. 13). The pine marten has an often undivided white throat-patch (called a 'bib'),

which is tinted with orange, a lustrous brown coat and a very bushy tail. The pattern of the marten's bib, like the weasel's belly pattern, is distinctive for each individual and can be used to help identify animals. Martens are regarded as the shyest of all the small mustelids.

Although pine martens are excellent climbers, they spend less time in trees than one would expect, often moving on the ground. They can swim, but rarely do so, although they are reported to attempt to catch fish from the edges of streams and ponds. They are considered to be nocturnal, but may be active by day. Martens frequently move in a zig-zag pattern which has been associated with searching for prey and possibly avoiding predatory birds. They commonly track their prey probably by scent, but they also ambush, rob nests and will dig up prey in burrows.

In these islands pine martens, if seen in trees, cannot be mistaken for anything else, for they are much bigger than squirrels. On the ground, however, a pine marten could be mistaken for a polecat or a mink; it can be distinguished from a polecat because of the polecat's distinctive face markings, whereas martens have uniform coloured chocolate brown faces and white lined ears. The differences between mink and martens are less straightforward, but the very bushy tail of the marten, in comparison with the narrower, more pointed tail of the mink, is a good indication to look for. Mink sometimes have white throat-marks (similar to those of the pine marten), but they are usually very irregular and normally white without an orange tint. Martens are squarer, more solid animals, without the sinuous narrowness of the mink and polecat. They are also higher on their legs than both mink and polecat.

On the European mainland, there is another marten species called the beech marten. This species is similar to the pine marten but has a pure white, untinted throat-bib, clearly divided into right and left halves. The beech marten is a creature of rocky open areas and is much less shy than ours, being frequently found in towns and villages, unlike the pine marten. It used to be thought that beech martens occurred in Britain but it is now known they are not present. However, at least two beech martens have escaped from zoos and wildlife parks in Britain and one managed to remain at large for nine months before being trapped.

Smaller than both pine marten and beech marten is another marten species that is now found only in Russia, the sable. Famous for its soft, long-haired coat, it is probably the most highly prized of all the fur-bearers. It is distinguished from other martens by its small size and by having an indistinct white throat-bib. There are two American marten species, the American marten itself, which is very like the pine marten, and

Pine marten in tree.

the fisher, which is the largest of all the martens. Fishers can weigh up to 5.5 kilograms (12 pounds) the weight of a small otter. Fisher is a highly inappropriate name for this animal, as it does not fish. The name is possibly derived from the French names *'fiche'*, *'ficheux'* or *'fichet'* for polecat fur. The most distinctive aspects about fishers, apart from their valuable frosted fur, is that they prey on porcupines (see Relations with man). Both these martens are still found over much of North America.

As important fur-bearers, the martens have all been hunted for their pelts by man for centuries. This exploitation and, at the same time, widespread destruction of their habitats has led to dramatic declines of martens, particularly in Europe, so that now vast areas of their former ranges are sadly devoid of these animals.

In Britain, pine martens were formerly found all over the mainland and on several offshore islands. However, by 1900, they were confined to a few small areas of the North of England and Northern Scotland. This was probably due to habitat destruction as well as direct persecution by gamekeepers. Birds of prey including buzzards, kites, ravens and harriers declined at around the same time. The situation for martens is more or less the same today (see map), although there has been an increase in their range in Scotland. In Ireland, the story was different, with martens

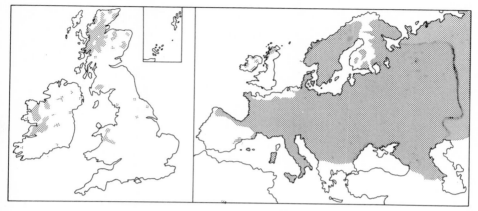

Distribution of pine marten.

remaining scattered but locally abundant until the 1950s. At that time changes in agricultural practices reduced their range dramatically to a few small areas in the east and some strongholds in the west (see map), notably the hazel woodlands of County Clare.

The most remarkable feature of martens, apart from their much sought-after fur, is their varied diet. Though they are carnivorous, they regularly eat all sorts of other items including berries, rosehips, crab-apples, nuts, earthworms and insects. Their staple diet is birds and small mammals, the more varied fruits and nuts being eaten only when they are easily available.

The martens of Dromore Wood

Dromore Wood is a mixed woodland of about 140 hectares (346 acres) in County Clare, Ireland, owned by the state. It has a resident population of about ten martens (that is a relatively high density) and these were studied by Irish scientists in the 1970s. What they discovered was that martens rarely ventured into the open, preferring dense cover. They traversed a system of regularly used pathways within cover. They spent a good deal of their time on the ground, on paths which were marked by their scats (droppings). The scats were left in obvious positions, enabling the scientists to collect them at regular weekly intervals. The scats were analysed in order to ascertain the marten's diet. The overall results are presented in the chapter on Food (pp. 73 and 74). But the abridged table of food eaten does not do justice to the varied delicacies they enjoyed in this relatively rich lowland wood. They ate large quantities of birds, including ducks, pigeons, waders and their eggs. They ate wood mice, rabbits, hares and a few shrews, squirrels and even a stoat.

They also ate beetles, frogs, lizards, bees, earwigs and snails. Eighty per cent of the droppings had earthworm remains in them. In season they ate quantities of wild berries, nuts and crab-apples. Truely an omnivorous diet. They share this beautiful wood with foxes, badgers, stoats, hares, red squirrels, mice, shrews and hedgehogs.

Habitats

A habitat is a combination of things that make up the most suitable environment for that animal: those things include prey species, predators, climate, den sites, vegetation and water supply. Some aspects may be more important than others, for example, for small mustelids prey availability and den sites are high on the list. Understanding its habitat preferences is vital to understanding any animal.

All small mustelids live in a variety of habitats, but each species has a specific range of preferences. Weasels live in habitats that include urban areas, lowland pasture and woodland, amongst others. On mainland Britain, they are virtually ubiquitous, needing only a little cover and sufficient prey to survive. They are adept at exploiting temporarily available habitats, hence their occurrence in new urban areas. In such areas they should play a very beneficial role in controlling rats and mice.

Stoats similarly can occur in a wide variety of habitats, but they do not occur with weasels in urban areas in England. They survive better at high altitudes and moorland than weasels, probably because their principal prey (rabbits) are better at surviving at such altitudes than the weasel's principal prey (small mammals). Stoats are also much commoner on offshore islands probably for reasons explained earlier (see p. 24), and ability to deal with a wider range of prey than weasels. So weasels and stoats occur most often in places where their favourite prey is most often found, and which offer the best cover.

It is interesting that in Ireland, where there are no weasels, stoats are sometimes found in urban areas; perhaps there is some competition between weasels and stoats, which, in Britain, favours the weasels. In Britain, weasels and, to a lesser extent, stoats, are found in woodland, as are the small mustelids (stoats and weasels) in New Zealand. The frequent occurrence of stoats in New Zealand's woodlands and to a lesser extent in British and Irish woodlands conflicts with what has been reported from elsewhere in the stoat's range. In Asia, North America and mainland Europe, for example, stoats are reported to avoid forests. This could be due to competition from some other animal in the forests of Eurasia and North America which is absent in the forests of the three islands Britain, Ireland and New Zealand. In New Zealand, all three species, polecat, stoat and weasel, are found together in scrub and native grassland habitats. Polecats are absent from woodlands. Stoats occur at all altitudes, but, as in Britain, weasels are scarce or absent in upland habitats.

Polecats in Europe are found in woodland, being reportedly most numerous in broad-leaved or mixed forest. They are thought to prefer river valleys where there would be an abundance of mammal, bird, reptile and amphibian prey. However in Britain, at least, this reported preference for valley floors could be a reflection of the fact that most British polecats are now found in Wales. As most roads there are on valley floors, and these are the focus for sighting and road casualty records of polecats, this apparent preference may say more about the observers than the polecats. In Britain, polecats are also reported from farmland, sea cliffs and sand dune areas but are said to be absent from populated areas. Nevertheless, they can be found on the edge of towns and will den in or near farm buildings and houses, particularly in winter (see Denning).

Pine martens prefer woodland, preferably mature; however, in parts of Scotland and Ireland they inhabit bare rocky hills, moorland and sometimes even seashore. Recent research in Scotland has identified mixed conifer plantations as favoured marten habitat. The recent reafforestation in Scotland and Ireland has provided additional marten habitat but as this is usually unbroken coniferous woodland, usually regularly cleaned up, it is of limited value to martens. Studies of North American martens using radiotracking have identified tall, dense forest, often coniferous, near meadows and rivers, and with plenty of stumps and logs, as preferred habitat. Clearly an essential part of marten habitat is secure den sites (see Denning), as well as the availability of plentiful prey and other foods. Beech martens, unlike pine martens, are found in built-up areas, where, like weasels, they have a beneficial role as they prey on rats and mice.

Stoats in island habitats — a success?

Stoats colonize offshore islands readily and are commonly reported from islands off Britain, Ireland, New Zealand and the Soviet Union. Analysis of the occurrence of small mustelids on major British offshore islands has shown that islands smaller than 90 square kilometres (35 square miles) support no resident small mustelids (with the apparent exception of Guernsey, which once was reported to have had stoats); bigger islands under 380 square kilometres (147 square miles) support only stoats, no weasels (e.g. Jersey, Islay and Jura). There are good reasons for this. Stoats are able swimmers (they are reported to swim up to 1,200 metres/1,300 yards) in the sea to reach islands off New Zealand); the females are rarely not fertilized (see p. 55) and they can survive on a wide variety of food. They were introduced to the Dutch island of Terschelling, with weasels, in 1931 to control water voles. They increased prodigiously and still survive whereas the weasels and water voles are now extinct. Their success on offshore islands is a mixed blessing as they often kill colonial sea birds and in New Zealand they pose a special threat to native birds (see Conservation). On New Zealand's offshore islands many of its unique native birds survive after they have become rare or extinct on the mainland; these birds are vulnerable to stoats. One such island is Adele Island off New Zealand's South Island. It is small, 87 hectares (⅓ square mile), yet unlike most British offshore islands of that size, stoats thrive there in the native scrub and on the beaches. Stoats had reached a relatively high density there when they were all trapped and removed in 1981. Since then, despite the fact that the island is 800 metres (870 yards) from the mainland, about two stoats a year arrive. Considerable sustained efforts would be needed to exclude them, so they continue to pose a threat to the native birds.

Relations with each other

How do these animals interact with each other? Both with members of their own species and members of other species? These are, in my opinion, the most exciting and interesting questions that can be asked about their ecology. Unfortunately, up to now, very few facts have been available.

Apart from when they are breeding (see pp. 55-58), they are usually solitary and to a greater or lesser extent territorial. As they need large quantities of prey, their territories are, in comparison to these animals' size, vast, so that they cannot actively defend them. Instead, it is believed that they mark the boundaries with anal scent gland secretions and sometimes urine to let other members of their own species know that the territory is taken.

The males, being bigger, have bigger territories than females; a male may have one, or more, female territories within his own (see drawing). Males defend their territories against other males. Females defend theirs against other females. This behaviour is called 'intra-sexual territoriality'. The male mates with females on his patch, which is technically called a 'dispersed harem system'. These territories are not static or indeed totally exclusive; they may wander in and out of each other's territories. Boundaries of territories change with the season, the quantity of prey available or due to the death of a neighbour. Pine martens and polecats have been observed fighting in the wild, possibly over territory. Both stoats and weasels have a more or less stable territorial system which is believed to break up in the spring with males then ranging more widely probably in anticipation of breeding. Martens appear to have the most stable territories of all, using the same boundaries year in, year out.

However, in Finnish Lapland in the far north of Europe, martens have been reported to live without any apparent territories in winter. In this cold, barren habitat groups of martens have been reported feeding together on carrion such as reindeer carcasses. There is no evidence of aggressive encounters, territorial defence or use of scent marks as territorial markers. It has been suggested that this is because in such an unpredictable habitat they would need such a huge territory that it would be too costly to defend. This social system of no territories has been referred to as 'martelism' and may well yet be found in other species of small mustelids in unpredictable habitats.

In normal habitats, those young animals that fail to secure a territory in

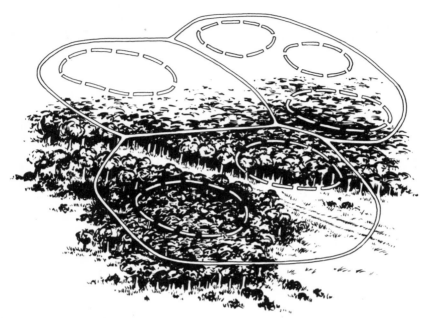

Male (solid lines) *and female* (broken lines) *territories in woodland, an example of intra-sexual territoriality.*

adequate terrain are very much at risk and are likely to survive only if a neighbour with a territory in adequate habitat is killed, enabling them to take over. Such animals are usually males, they are unlikely to mate and are probably more at risk from predators than animals with territories. In this fashion such animals provide a reserve population.

Between each species some competition would be expected as they all, more or less, take the same prey: small mammals and birds. Stoats and weasels, for example, are very similar in size, shape and diet; therefore, why does not one outcompete the other? The co-existence of weasels and stoats in the same habitat has long puzzled ecologists. It is said that weasels avoid contact with stoats, so that stoats are unaware of them. However, such behaviour would still not explain why one did not dominate in a competitive situation for competition will occur even if the animals are unaware of each other.

In Canada, it has been claimed that the long-tail weasel (see p. 18) does limit the distribution of the weasel and the stoat there. The northern limits of the long-tail weasel are determined by snow cover. Where there are no long-tail weasels, and just weasels and stoats, it has been suggested that, in Canada at least, they avoid competition by hunting different prey in different habitats. But, in contradiction of that, in Britain, stoats and weasels appear to occur in the same habitats and hunt the same prey, so they surely must compete? This is backed up by two interesting observations: firstly, when the rabbit disease myxomatosis swept through Britain in 1954 removing 99 per cent of rabbits — an important prey for both weasels and stoats — the aftermath had dramatic effects on the number of weasels and stoats. Weasels were caught in record numbers in the post-1954 period indicating that they benefited, whereas stoat numbers were dramatically down on previous years. This suggests that weasels can, and probably do, outcompete stoats in the absence of rabbits, as they are better adapted to feed on small rodents. However, the removal of rabbits made more grazing available to voles and mice, swelling their numbers, which would have helped weasels, let alone the fact that there were fewer stoats.

Secondly, on British offshore islands, where voles are often absent and there are fewer prey species, stoats occur commonly but weasels rarely. This suggests that stoats compete better than weasels in the difficult situations provided by island environments where there are fewer small rodent species.

Since 1929, American mink have been escaping from fur farms and establishing feral (wild breeding) populations in Britain and Ireland. The spread of these introduced carnivores led to concern about their impact on smaller native animals, including stoats and weasels. However mink appear to have established themselves without causing the decline of stoats and weasels.

We know little of the interactions between martens, polecats and other small mustelids. In Ireland, it is known that stoats survive in marten habitat (see Martens, p. 40). It is likely that in some circumstances martens and polecats could compete, but this may be avoided by different habitat preferences.

Which stoat is dominant?

Animals are not all equal. In terms of social organization, one animal, usually the bigger and stronger, and always the territory holder, will dominate others. The 'top-dog' animal will harass an 'under-dog' animal, chasing it away and often stealing the under-dog's prey. In

Sweden, the social organization of stoats was investigated in a series of experiments. Adult mature males always dominated juvenile males and females outside the breeding season. However, in March and April, the time that females are pregnant, this changed and females were definitely becoming equally dominant with the much bigger males. This is probably an adaptation to help females defend their young and have better access to prey. A similar change occurs in social organizations of breeding weasels and otters.

So, BY SIMPLY SIMULATING PREGNANCY WE SEE THAT THE SMALLER FEMALE GAINS SUDDEN AND DRAMATIC DOMINANCE OVER THE LARGER MALE

Relations with man

Apart from their prey and each other, man is probably the most important animal with which small mustelids interact. Man has influenced most of the environments where these animals live and man's activities have led to both decreases and increases in their populations. For example, by introducing prey such as rats and rabbits, man has inadvertently probably allowed an increase in the numbers of stoats.

Certain small mustelids are killed systematically for their fur or because of their alleged damage to poultry or game birds. Every year literally millions of wild small mustelids are killed for their fur. This sometimes has no apparent effect on the populations, but other times, particularly with the martens and polecats, such activities have led to local extinctions and dramatic declines.

Probably the most highly prized fur of all is that of the sable, followed by the white winter fur of the stoat, which is called ermine. In feudal times

HAVE YOU NOTICED HOW THE HIGHER THEIR RANK THE MORE RANK THE ANIMAL THEY WEARS!

there were strict laws governing who could wear the furs of certain mammals, according to social status. For example the King or Queen could wear ermine (and royalty still do wear ermine on ceremonial occasions), but peasants had to make do with the fur of cats or rabbits.

Trappers who hunted small mustelids were the first white men to explore the far north of both North America and Eurasia. A good deal of information about small mustelids has come down to us from these trappers, because to successfully take wild animals you have to be knowledgeable about their habits. Nevertheless, like all such lore, some of these trappers' and hunters' tales are good stories, but have no basis in fact. Examples of such stories often refer to the fearlessness of these animals. The trappers, for example, tell tales of pairs of weasels returning to the corpse of a young animal to retrieve and bury it, or to avenge themselves on its killers.

The rise of game estates in Britain and Ireland in the last century led to extensive planting of woodland as game cover and to persecution of small mustelids and other predators. In some areas the preservation of woods for hunting and game-bird cover undoubtedly provided habitats for small mustelids. On the other hand, gamekeepers trap, shoot and poison all alleged predators of game birds. This can and sometimes does mean all predators. The wisdom of this is questionable, for although some predators will undoubtedly kill game birds, they also kill such pests as rats, mice and rabbits. It is not uncommon for game estates to have problems with rats and rabbits, probably as the result of predator control.

Polecats and martens are now rare in Britain and one of the factors that was important in their decline was persecution by gamekeepers. Martens are now fully protected, but polecats are not. Their only protection is that the law in Britain says they can only be killed using a non-automatic weapon. But given that they are so rare, should they be killed at all? Stoats and weasels are common and have withstood persistent persecution by gamekeepers. There are ecological reasons for this (see next chapter). Their main prey are rabbits, rats, voles and mice, and, unless they enter a game-bird rearing pen, they are unlikely to kill adult game birds. As long as a gamekeeper's rearing pens are proofed to prevent entry by stoats and weasels, there is little cause to kill them either.

Gamekeepers feel a need to show their employers that they are doing their job. They often display the bodies of the predators they kill on a fence by the roadside so that their employers can see the results of their work. Such lines are called 'gibbit' lines. There are often several weasels and stoats among the carcasses (see drawing on next page). The gibbit line

A gamekeeper's gibbet.

is in fact a grisly hangover from the days when dead people were hung by city gates and by roadsides as a warning to others.

An important tool of gamekeepers in the past was the gin trap, a cruel, toothed leg-hold trap (see drawing). These traps are very efficient and are still used by fur trappers in other parts of the world. When caught in such traps animals in desperation frequently bite their own legs off to escape. Clearly it is a good thing that such barbaric traps are now banned. The word 'gin' comes from 'engin' which was a countryman's word for any gadget that worked without the immediate presence of man. Today gamekeepers often use Fenn traps for stoats and weasels. These are set in small tunnels and usually kill the trapped animal instantly. Most keepers have such traps set at various points on their 'beat'. As the gamekeeper inspects the traps daily he gets to know his beat very well and this is probably more important for the preservation of game than any effect on remaining small mustelids.

Apart from killing small mustelids, man has also influenced their populations by introductions. For example, in Britain (admittedly some centuries ago) man introduced rabbits and rats, and these now form a large part of the diet of British small mustelids. On the other hand the deliberate introduction of small mustelids to New Zealand to control rabbits may also have caused declines in native species of birds there (see Conservation).

Legally, in Britain today stoats and weasels are not protected. An analysis of the historic decline of polecats and martens indicates that direct persecution did play a role in that decline and that therefore their legal protection is worthwhile. In the Irish Republic, both stoats and martens are protected, and in Northern Ireland martens are protected.

What of the future? Man has altered the environment and it is therefore up to man to manage it as it now is. One of the most exciting suggestions for such management is the re-introduction to suitable areas of the larger, rarer small mustelids such as polecats and martens (see p. 105). The story of the American fisher (see box) is an inspiring example of successful re-introduction.

An ermine in a gin trap.

Fishers and porcupines

Porcupines are large rodents equipped with long sharp quills, not unlike hedgehogs, but not in fact related to them. In North America porcupines are a serious pest, damaging trees, buildings and even telephone lines, by gnawing. Because of their quills, they are rarely killed by other animals. The only predator capable of regularly killing them is the fisher, the largest of all the martens (see pp. 37 and 38).

Due to trapping for their fur and habitat destruction, fishers declined rapidly at the end of the last century and the beginning of this one. This is likely to have led to an increase in porcupines, which in turn led to increased damage, and lots of unobtainable telephone calls! In the more enlightened era since 1950, widespread and successful re-introductions of fishers have taken place all over North America to control porcupines. This is a fine example of man redressing ecological damage. Similar re-introductions of martens in various areas of Britain to control grey squirrels have been suggested.

Ecological roles

Each small mustelid has a different way in which it has adapted to its environment, part of what is called an 'ecological strategy'. These strategies range from the long-life, slow-breeding one of the martens, which is in response to a stable environment, to the short-life, fast-breeding one of the weasels, which enables them to thrive in almost any environment.

Martens mature late, probably at about the age of 2, live a long time (up to 18 years) and have a single small litter of 2-4 young each year. They occur in mature woodland. Polecats mature quicker than martens and can breed in the year after birth but they do not live such a long time (up to 14 years). They can have two litters in a year of 4-5 young. Polecats are not as fussy about habitat as martens (see Habitats).

Stoats have only a single litter each year, but this can be of up to 12 young. They do not live as long as polecats (up to 7 years) and they cannot breed until their second year. Stoats occur in almost any habitat where sufficient cover is available. Weasels are the fastest breeders of the lot, maturing in their first year and often having two litters per year of 4-6 young. They do not live very long in the wild — a 3-year-old weasel is exceptional. Weasels can thrive in almost any habitat where there is sufficient prey and cover.

The diagram shows how habitat, breeding rate and longevity interrelate for the four species. The weasel is able to quickly exploit a temporary surplus of small mammals by producing a lot of offspring, whereas in a predictable mature woodland the marten is admirably adapted to producing an adequate number of young.

It is impossible for a large quantity of mature woodland to appear all at once, therefore martens would never need to produce a lot of offspring to take advantage of this. They therefore produce a small but adequate number to colonize new habitats that might be available.

Another aspect of ecological adaptation among small mustelids is among the sexes. The males are always much bigger than the females and this is referred to as 'sexual dimorphism'. The difference in size of each sex of the British small mustelids is illustrated here (see diagram). Perhaps the most dramatic difference between the sexes in such animals is in the weight of American fishers. The female can weigh 2 kilograms (4 lb), whereas the male can be 5.5 kilograms (12 lb).

Why are the sexes such different sizes? Ecologists have long believed that this is an adaptation that allows the sexes to share the same area and avoid competing for prey. It is known from some studies that males and females do take slightly different proportions of prey species. However not all studies confirm this and given the conflicting evidence another idea has been put forward to explain sexual dimorphism.

This more sophisticated idea is called the Erlinge-Moors hypothesis (a scientific idea yet to be proved) after the two researchers who proposed it independently. They argued that females were smaller so that they could conserve their energy costs while bringing up young, and to allow them access to the burrows of small mammals. Certainly there is no doubt that during the breeding season females do need considerable quantities of energy and need to find it in a small area. However, the idea relies on calculations of an invented male-sized female and does not fully explain the range of sexual dimorphism found in nature. Studies of energetics of fishers (see Energetics) support the Erlinge-Moors hypothesis, however.

Sexual dimorphism in British small mustelids — from average body measurements (in millimetres)

	Male	Female
Weasel	204	180
Stoat	297	264
Polecat	380	335
Marten	507	439

Ecological strategies in small mustelids

Marten	Polecat	Stoat	Weasel

Stable habitat .... ⟷ .... ⟷ .... Unstable habitat

Slow reproduction .... ⟷ .... ⟷ ..... Rapid reproduction

Small litters .... ⟷ .... ⟷ .... Large litters

Large body .... ⟷ .... ⟷ .... Small body

Long life span .... ⟷ .... ⟷ .... Short life span

Breeding

Small mustelids display an interesting range of breeding arrangements, of which the stoat's reproductive biology has attracted the most attention and is perhaps the most bizarre. Stoats mate in summer, the males being fertile from about March until around August. Young stoats are born in March or April. What is bizarre is that young female stoats, possibly with their eyes not yet opened and unweaned, are fertilized in the nest by the males. This is usually the resident male who is also likely to mate with their mother and may often be their father. This is why to call a man 'a bit of a stoat' is considered such an insult.

When a female stoat is fertilized the resultant embryo travels down to the womb. There it stays until the following spring when it implants and active pregnancy begins. This curious phenomenon is called 'delayed implantation'. Delayed implantation also occurs in martens, badgers, fishers and many other mammals.

What about the father/daughter mating in stoats? Why does it not lead to problems related to inbreeding? We do not know the answer. One explanation is that because stoats do not live long, the male that has mated with the mother the previous summer is very often replaced by another the following summer, thus avoiding father/daughter matings. Ovulation (the shedding of the egg in females) in stoats is induced, which means that mating stimulates the production of the egg. It is probable that ovulation in the other small mustelids is similarly induced.

Mating behaviour in small mustelids appears to be noisy, vigorous and lengthy. In martens the females make a clucking noise before copulation and during copulation both sexes purr and growl a great deal. The male drags the female about by the neck (charming behaviour) and the whole thing often lasts more than an hour. Happily most marten matings occur on the ground, as the results of such behaviour in trees could be dangerous. Female martens are very adventurous and will travel to mate several times with various males.

Polecats behave in much the same way when mating; there's a great deal of chattering; the male polecat also grasps the female's neck and drags her about. Again copulation can last a long time, up to an hour. However the longest time spent in copulation among small mustelids is recorded for the domestic ferret and black-footed ferret, which will copulate for up to 3½ hours. It is likely that these elaborate proceedings have to do with

inducing ovulation in the female. Weasels indulge in a high-pitched trilling noise during mating. Scent glands probably play a role in courtships and mating of weasels — and all small mustelids.

In captive small mustelids some odd sexual behaviour has been recorded. When young polecats males will mount both males and females and females will do likewise in a form of aggressive play. In adult polecats a female has been observed to mount a male, but this was probably more aggressive than sexual behaviour. Adult female American martens will mount males when they are in season as will adult female stoats. However, it ought to be remembered that odd behaviour is often recorded in captive animals and may have more to do with the stress of captivity than the animal's natural instincts. Such behaviour has not been observed in wild small mustelids.

So the common factors between small mustelid breeding are induced ovulation and elaborate mating behaviour, which is probably linked to inducing that ovulation. Two of the British small mustelids, stoats and martens, used delayed implantation, which is one reason for thinking that they may be more closely related than is currently accepted. Another breeding characteristic among small mustelids which suggests that martens and stoats are closely related is the structure of the baculum or *os penis*. The baculum is a bone that is part of the penis of small mustelids and many other mammals. It is useful to feel for this bone (which is normally concealed in the body) if you are in doubt about the sex of a mustelid. The bacula of martens and stoats are made up of bones joined together and grooved, but not hooked. However, the bacula of polecats and weasels are also joined, grooved and hooked, rather like a hockey stick! (see diagram). These facts about breeding make for interesting suggestions about how small mustelids are related, nevertheless a great deal more research needs to be done to find out the truth about such interrelations.

In a population of small mustelids, do all the animals breed? The answer

A pair of polecats.

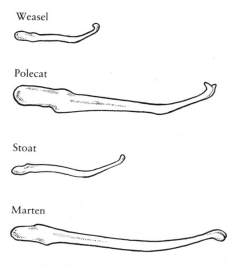

Weasel

Polecat

Stoat

Marten

Bacula of British small mustelids.

is probably not. There is evidence that some males, despite being the correct age for maturity, are not fertile and do not therefore reproduce. These are likely to be under-dog males confined to habitats with poor quality and quantity of prey and cover. Females on the other hand usually do breed. It is old ferreting lore that if female ferrets do not breed every year they will die. While not strictly true, female ferrets will be out of condition should they not breed and therefore more prone to die. It is not known if this is also true of wild small mustelid females.

Growing up

Small mustelid mothers rear their young on their own, without any assistance from the father or other relatives. This puts a considerable strain on the mother and is considered to be very important in the overall ecology of these animals. There are two principal reasons why this is considered important. First, it is likely that females have adapted for this critical period of rearing the young, by being smaller, and therefore having less energy demands than the bigger male. Secondly for the young themselves, the quantity of food — at first milk and, when weaned, solid food — is critical for their survival and probably their overall size. It is known that like most mammals small mustelids grow rapidly while in the care of their mother and this period of growth is considered likely to determine their eventual size.

As the food brought by the small mustelid mother to the young in the breeding den must be carried, the availability of suitably portable foods is likely to be critical. Weasels can carry small rodents and nestling young rodents. Stoats carry small rodents but also carry young rabbits. However, an adult rabbit would be too big to take back to the nest. Birds's eggs may also be carried but there are difficulties in carrying them. Stoats in New Zealand have been observed taking large gull eggs. They attacked the eggs at the pointed end. As the eggs were too big to carry entirely in the mouth the stoats sank their teeth into the egg and tucked it in between the forelegs and moved forwards with the egg in that position. Often nestling birds, which, like eggs, are available at the right time of year, are taken by stoats to their young. Polecats and martens have less of a problem carrying prey because of their larger size. Because breeding dens are difficult to find and to observe, we know little about the frequency of feeding of the young on prey in the wild.

The young small mustelids (called kits or kittens) are born blind and naked or thinly furred. The maternal nest is a secure but usually a non-permanent affair. It is often the former nest of a prey animal such as a rat or squirrel which may well have been eaten before the takeover. Sometimes the nest is lined with the fur of several small mammal prey. Occasionally, the nest has no lining whatsoever and there are reports of marten kits being found in bare rocky crevices. The kits are helpless for the first weeks of life during which they may be moved to another nest, particularly if the original nest is disturbed. This is a dangerous time for both mother and kits for they are both very vulnerable to predators and the mother may lose one kit, or more, during the move.

Young stoats appear to have a special adaptation for such moves. At about three weeks old a mane of long dense fur develops on the upper neck (see drawing) which may be to enable the mother to carry them with greater ease. This mane may also have something to do with scent glands (see Smells). Another danger faced by mother and kits is cannibalism. It is not uncommon: the eating of young stoats in the nest by other adults has been reported from both wild and captive animals in both Britain and Ireland. Captive small mustelid mothers will often also cannibalize their own young, but this is probably abnormal behaviour produced by the stress of captivity and disturbance (see Captive and tame small mustelids). This is a sad phenomenon which makes captive breeding (see Conservation) very difficult.

Moves of the maternal nest may not always result from disturbance. It has been suggested that such moves are to enable the mother (and later the young) to exploit various areas of their home range, thereby getting access to more prey. The change in dominance behaviour, when the breeding female becomes dominant to the father, at least equally dominant (see pp. 46 and 47) also helps, by enabling the female and her family use of a bigger area of the male's home range than would be usual.

The eyes of weasel kits are open by about 3 to 4 weeks, roughly the same time as they are weaned. However, they may continue to get milk for some time after weaning. The young weasels can kill prey at 6 to 8 weeks.

A young stoat.

Young polecats playing: note the open mouth.

Although this is an instinctive, not learnt, skill they probably become more adept at it as they grow up. When in family groups, in summer and autumn, weasels are reported to attack large prey such as squirrels and birds which they would never attack on their own.

Young stoats open their eyes at 4 to 6 weeks, the females being first to open theirs. This may be due to the fact that female stoat kits mate when very young. They begin to eat solid food at the same time and by week 6 or 7 the black tip has appeared on their tails. The appearance of the black tip coincides with their first independent ventures outside the nest. Young stoats and other small mustelids remain with their mother for some time more and the family will hunt together as a 'pack'. These groups of mother and young have given rise to tales of packs of stoats that are occasionally reported to attack larger animals, even dogs and people. Young stoats can kill prey at about 10 weeks and, like all the small mustelids this behaviour is instinctive rather than learnt; there is little doubt that practice makes perfect. Young stoats and weasels use a wrap-around technique to trap mice prey using both fore and hind feet (see drawing on p. 23). Young fishers are reported to use the same technique for hares.

Polecat kits, like those of stoats and weasels, have their eyes open at about 5 weeks. Subsequently, the males grow faster than females and the same appears to be true for stoats and weasels. At this phase of life the difference in size between the sexes occurs. The young polecats can kill instinctively at about the same time, killing in the usual mustelid way by biting the prey at the base of the neck.

The play of young polecats has been studied using cine film and this has shown us a good deal about play. Play is difficult for scientists to define, but is essentially 'make believe' non-serious behaviour. It is common among most young mammals, having been observed, for example, in rats, whales and chimpanzees.

Play simulates real behaviour, so you get play-fighting, play-predation and play-signals. Young polecats tell each other that their play is not to be taken seriously in various ways, the most frequent of which is the play-face, which is a relaxed open mouth face (see drawing). This type of play-face is common in young carnivores and primates. The play-face is constantly repeated and happens during about half the time polecats spend playing. A polecat playing being chased will look behind to see if it is being pursued and at the same time make a play-face.

Play in polecats, as in many other mammals, is characterized by exaggerated jerky movements which are never seen in real life. This will have been noticed by anyone who has seen a puppy or kitten playing. In play-fighting, if there is an obvious inequality between the polecats, the stronger will handicap itself in order that play can proceed. Should one or another animal get hurt, play abruptly ends with a squeal, cry or squeak. Life is again serious, there are no more play-faces or jerky movements. A number of different play behaviours have been described in polecats. For example in play-fighting there is: aim bite, bite (inhibited); nip; cuff with paw; roll over; kick; wrestle; lunge; stand over and mount. Play movements are also important and there is a great deal of chasing, following, pouncing and stalking.

The same sort of play has been observed in all small mustelid kits; it has been best studied in polecats because they are often kept in captivity (see Captive and tame small mustelids). It is likely to be vital for the physical and behavioural development of the young animals and it is of interest that play-chases get longer as young polecats get older, indicating a learning process. Play is not wholly confined to young animals. There is a certain amount of play behaviour during courtship. Captive female polecats, for example, will roll over and play-bite their mates when not on heat. However, play aside, while the young are in the nest, the mother polecat will defend her kits unhesitatingly whatever the size of the attacker.

Pine marten kits are the slowest of all the small mustelids to develop. Their eyes do not open until 32-38 days. They are weaned at 6-7 weeks, but are unable to kill proficiently until about 2½ months. They do not achieve full independence until about 6 months and will live in a family group until then. Slowly, as the kits get older, aggressive behaviour begins between the kits and also their mother. This usually occurs over food,

Young martens emerging from a den.

which by this time may be getting scarce. It is such aggression that is thought to trigger dispersion.

Dispersing

Why does an animal disperse? There are two principal reasons. The animal can be evicted, or it can move voluntarily. It is most likely that young animals are usually evicted by their parents or other immediate relatives. This allows the parents to maintain their usual territory. However, in short-lived species, such as stoats and weasels, the parents are quite often dead by the time the young mature, allowing some of them to settle on the parental area.

However, some dispersion will also be voluntary. It is known that some mammals, for example rats and rabbits, will occasionally wander far from their home area simply exploring. Sometimes the animal will not return, but will settle in a new area. Lack of, or a decline in, a resource such as prey or cover could prompt such voluntary movements. There are tales of mass movements of weasels and stoats which, it is suggested, are caused by cycles in the numbers of prey; this would be an example of voluntary dispersal. Martens in Lapland are known to explore new areas, usually if the supply of prey on their home area is poor. However, so far north in winter strict territories cease to exist and 'martelism' (see Relations with each other) prevails. Wandering outside the home area is not so exceptional under such conditions.

There have been two important studies, one in Sweden and one in Switzerland, about dispersion of the stoat. The Swedish and Swiss scientists studied dispersion in stoats as part of a larger study of stoat population dynamics. The stoat populations lived in a marshy farmland area in southern Sweden called Revinge and in valleys in the Jura mountains in Switzerland. Water voles were the main prey in both study sites. Revinge had lots of stone walls and was in use as a military training ground at the time which must have livened up the field work! The Swiss site in the Jura mountain valleys was mixed habitat with important peat bog sites.

The Swedish stoats at Revinge were found to have a definite pattern of dispersion. Young females usually settled on their parents' territory and rarely dispersed further. The young males, however, having spent the autumn and winter on, or near, their parents' home area would move extensively in the spring. After that the males that established themselves on areas with females usually stayed put, but those with no females and usually poor habitats, the 'under-dogs', continued to travel. The movements were, not surprisingly, considered to be determined by istribution of females. Two of the under-dog males were run over by ehicles, which today is probably a common fate of such surplus males, ue to the fact that they are moving around so much. Some males covered xtensive areas in summer — probably to find females.

In the Swiss study, two stoat populations were studied, one in an area vhere prey (water voles) was scarce and one where such prey was ommon. In the area where prey was scarce, the territorial system broke lown and all the males became travellers, females moving out of their ·arents' home areas but settling in very small areas of good habitat, 1amely peat bogs. In the area where water voles were common a similar ·attern of territories and movements to that in Sweden was recorded. ·tudies of stoats in New Zealand and Canada have also identified a imilar pattern of dispersion.

Weasels probably have similar patterns of dispersion to stoats; 1owever, because they have two litters a year and the young females can ·reed in their first year, they are likely to disperse more rapidly. The requent existence of a second litter, coupled with the difference in size ·etween the sexes (see Ecological roles) are the factors that give rise to tories about two types of weasels: ordinary and pygmy weasels existing ·ide by side. In some rural areas such weasels are called 'minivers'.

Gamekeepers in Britain record surges of stoats and weasels in their traps vhich are thought to reflect seasonal patterns of dispersion of animals ·eeking new areas and often mates; surges of weasels occur in mid-April ınd late summer; those of stoats occur in July and in November and)ecember.

The gamekeeper's trap is not the only hazard faced by dispersing small mustelids. It is a dangerous time for the inexperienced animal. Predators vill pick off many during dispersion, as they will be in unfamiliar habitats ınd without sufficient knowledge of cover. Another risky situation, which ·ets worse year by year, is crossing of roads.

Studies of road casualties of Irish stoats and long-tailed weasels in North America both confirm that males are the most prominent victims; ındeed the American study produced only male victims. The same result is ·ecorded for trapped samples of small mustelids, in which there are also more males than females. The sex ratio of dead weasels from British game ·states is usually about 75 per cent male. This predominance of males is not considered to reflect a larger population of males, rather that males ıre likely to travel further both because they have bigger areas than females, and during the mating season will range widely looking for females. As supporting evidence, male road casualties peak during the mating season. Young and female Irish stoats are killed on the roads in large numbers, from June to September and November. This is sufficiently like the dates of surges of stoats reported by gamekeepers in Britain to suggest it is linked to the same phenomenon. The fact that female stoats are killed in large numbers during this time in Ireland may mean that they are ranging further in search of prey to feed their young.

There is little information on dispersion of martens or polecats in Britain. Live trapping of martens in Montana in North America revealed that young males actively disperse, like stoats. The American martens were recorded dispersing in March and August. British polecat records peak in four months of the year, from August to November, suggesting that these months are when young polecats are dispersing. Feral polecat/ferrets on the Isle of Man are reported to be killed frequently on the roads there, but it is not known if this is seasonal.

Road casualty stoat in Ireland.

Denning

Dens are important for small mustelids, as they provide somewhere safe from predators where the animal can rest and keep warm; keeping warm is a particular problem if you are small and elongated like stoats and weasels. Sometimes the fur of prey, such as mice and voles, is used to insulate winter dens. It is considered likely that, in certain habitats, dens are scarce or absent. This can lead to competition for dens, or sharing dens with other species. Weasels, polecats and martens have all been found denning in badger setts. So important is the provision of dens that a lack of them could account for the total absence of a small mustelid species from particular habitats. The trend in agriculture and forestry to plant a single species of crop or trees and to remove all irregularities in the habitat such as perimeter fences, fallen trees, rotting logs and ruined houses has led to less denning sites and cover being available.

In the state of Iowa in the United States, a study from 1925 to 1957 reported that the change from hayfields to continuous corn caused less dens and cover to be available for small mustelids. Similarly in Britain the change to single crops in huge fields over approximately the same period has resulted in a similar loss of den sites and cover on farmland. In Britain and Ireland martens have readily exploited the new coniferous forestry plantations in the last fifty years. However, such woodlands are relatively clean, neatly planted and rarely have trees of sufficient age to provide good big tree holes for martens' dens. The martens make do with dens in bird's nests or squirrel dreys and have been known to travel to find secure dens in a ruined house or old stone wall. It is possible that the supplying of artificial den sites (piles of large stones are acceptable) would encourage further colonization of these new forests by martens.

There are three basic types of small mustelid den: there is the maternal den, where young are born and reared; there is a sleeping den to which they return for prolonged periods, usually to sleep. Finally there are temporary dens or bolt holes which tend to be for emergency use and will be scattered all over the home range. These den types are not strictly differentiated, since a sleeping den may become a maternal den or vice versa, and the use of dens changes from day to day and from season to season. Usually an animal will have a number of sleeping dens dotted around its home range. The resident animal will live in each one for a few days, hunting around it, and then move on to another sleeping den.

The dens of weasels are often in mole runs or hills. Mole runs are the ideal size for weasels and provide useful underground pathways out of sight of predators. This sometimes leads to weasels being found in mole traps. Weasel dens can also be found in vole, mouse and shrew nests, farm buildings and, in North America in gopher and ground squirrel nests. They also occasionally den in rabbit burrows and bird's nests. The fleas they acquire reflect where they den (see Parasites). Weasels often line their dens with prey fur.

Stoats, being bigger, need bigger dens. They den in tree holes, bird's nests, holes in stone walls or banks, and commandeer prey burrows. In a study of Irish stoats, 19 sleeping den sites were identified: 9 were in common rat holes, 4 were in rabbit warrens, 4 were in piles of wood or stones, 1 was in a woodmouse burrow and 1 up a lime tree. Some of these may have been maternal dens. Clearly a mixed bag of den sites, however rat holes were by far the most common den site. This was reflected in the fleas found on the Irish stoats, which were principally rat fleas. In habitats where suitable prey burrows are not common stoats often den in piles of stones, which they seem to find particularly attractive.

Polecats do excavate their own dens but they also occupy the dens of prey species. The most frequently occupied prey burrow is that of the rabbit; however, the occurrence of hedgehog fleas on polecats suggests that they take over hedgehog nests from time to time. They have been found in fox dens and badger setts. Polecat sleeping dens can be quite complex, having more than one entrance, some food storage areas and sleeping and living chambers.

The maternal den will be lined with vegetation, normally grass and leaves; and unlike the sleeping den, it will have a single small opening. Periodically, like badgers, polecats will air the bedding by bringing it out and spreading it around. As the weather gets colder in winter polecats will often den in or near farms or other buildings, often in wood stacks.

Martens may have difficulty finding dens that are large enough and are attracted to ruined or even occupied buildings and stone walls because of their need for a secure den. In these islands they are known to den in rocky crevices, usually under one or more large rocks, in holes in river banks or peat cuttings, in tree holes or squirrel dreys and bird's nests (where they acquire bird and squirrel fleas).

In North America martens have a somewhat unique relationship with the North American species of red squirrel. During a radio-tracking study of martens in Alaska, 28 of 37 marten den sites were in red squirrel 'middens'. These middens are large long-lasting mounds, composed of bits of pine cones. They are used by the squirrels to store uneaten cones. It would appear that the Alaskan martens are often dependent on such middens for suitable den sites. The two species (squirrel and marten) appear to co-exist quite happily during the autumn and winter, both living in or around the midden. We don't have such middens in the British Isles.

Food

What do small mustelids eat? The answer is almost always other animals, except for martens, which regularly eat vegetable matter. This is one aspect of their ecology about which there is a reasonable amount of information, because it is relatively straightforward to identify food remains in their guts and droppings (see Scientific studies).

Weasels are considered to be specialists in feeding on small mammals

Weasel eating a mouse.

(voles and mice). The weasel's dependence on such prey is illustrated by increases in weasel numbers being associated with 'mouse years' (years when mice are abundant). The staple diet of stoats is considered to be mammals of rabbit/water vole size. We know from studies of diet that these generalizations are correct: results of findings about the diet of British stoats and weasels are illustrated in the table (p.74). On mainland Europe, the water vole is often the staple prey of stoats, just as it probably was in Britain prior to the introduction of rabbits and rats.

The rabbit is now the stoats' most regular food in Britain, Ireland and New Zealand. The dependence of stoats on rabbits was dramatically illustrated by a sharp decline in stoat numbers reported by gamekeepers in Britain after myxomatosis virtually wiped out rabbits in the 1950s. A similar decline in numbers of Irish stoats is also reckoned to have occurred. Stoats will occasionally eat poultry and small mammals, including shrews; practically all carnivores will avoid feeding on shrews, possible because shrews release some repellent chemical that makes them taste nasty. However, captive weasels and stoats in environments with little alternative prey, such as Ireland, have been known to eat shrews. This suggests that, if sufficiently hungry, small mustelids will eat them routinely.

Polecats eat a wide variety of mammal prey, including rabbits, rats, voles and mice; often mammal prey are young from a nest. They will also take poultry, wild birds and their eggs, amphibians (e.g. frogs), reptiles (i.e. snakes and lizards) and fish. Polecats will also take carrion and have been known to feed on dead badgers and other large mammal carrion.

Martens, however, are the most varied in their diet; they feed on carrion, live mammal and bird prey, beetles, fish, nuts, fungi, fruit and berries. The fruit and berries may appear strange for a carnivore, but badgers and, indeed, foxes also eat considerable quantities of fruit and berries when available. Some martens have also been reported feeding on bird tables and on bits of sandwiches left behind by forest workers. Martens' staple prey is small rodents and birds, with other foods making up variable proportions of the diet as available. Their diet, like the diet of all small mustelids, varies widely from habitat to habitat and from season to season. Take, for example, the recorded diet of martens in Irish and Scottish study sites (see pp. 73 and 74). On the Irish site, a lowland wood (Dromore Wood, Co. Clare, see pp. 39-40), birds were a major prey and mammals were comparatively minor. On the Scottish site, which was relatively open habitat, good for rabbits and field voles, mammals were a major part of the diet.

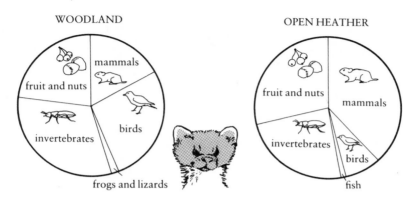

WOODLAND

OPEN HEATHER

Marten diet in two different habitats: Dromore Wood, Ireland (left) and Beinn Eighe, Scotland (right) – see chart on next page for details.

In Lapland, where marten territory ceases to exist and 'martelism' occurs (see Relations with each other) there are records of 3 or 4 martens feeding on the same deer carcass on the same night. This would never happen in areas where martens have established territories, so social and foraging behaviour, as well as diet, changes with habitat. It is well known that the diet of small mustelids is influenced by habitat, season and prey availability and, as we have seen, prey availablity has a dramatic influence on small mustelids. It is also evident from some studies that the diet of the sexes of small mustelids varies, the smaller females preying on smaller prey, but this is not always the case.

The most controversial aspect of the diet of stoats and weasels is whether or not they feed on game birds. The answer is, yes, sometimes they do, usually taking young game birds either from or near their nests. However, the influence such predation has on overall populations of adult game birds is frequently slight and certainly does not justify, in cost-benefit terms, continuous control measures against small mustelids. There is some evidence that short-term predator control, including killing small mustelids, does help partridge populations, but partridges are particularly vulnerable birds.

Should a small mustelid get into a game-rearing pen where the birds are confined and easily killed, all the birds in the pen may be killed, despite the fact that the predator could never possibly eat them all. This is called 'surplus killing' and is the result, not of a malicious streak in the character of the predator, but in the predator getting unnatural super-stimulus of available prey (confined birds: something that would not happen in the wild). Properly designed game-rearing facilities should include proofing against access by small mustelids, which is much more cost effective than trying to kill such predators. In any event, we know that gamekeepers mainly kill male stoats and weasels; therefore their efforts have little long-term effect on overall stoat and weasel populations. Sometimes game birds get their own back anyway. Twice dead stoats have been found beside nesting pheasants from which one can only conclude that the hen pheasants killed the stoats before they could raid the nest.

Such was not the case with polecats and martens, which were driven back to remote areas by persecution by gamekeepers. Was such persecution justified? Certainly both species would have raided game bird nests and, if they had access, would have been involved in surplus killing of confined game birds. However, if a game bird species, such as grouse, partridge or pheasant, or indeed any bird species, became as rare as polecats or martens, there would be a considerable outcry from some quarters. This enables one to draw some interesting conclusions about human value judgments on animals.

Percentage of major prey from various studies of the diet of British stoats and weasels

Prey	Stoat	Weasel
Rabbits and hares	34-56	0-22
Rats	0-3	0-14
Small mammals (including shrews)	6-29	43-76
Birds	12-41	10-28

Recorded marten diet from Irish and Scottish studies

	AREA	
	Dromore Wood Co Clare, Ireland (woodland)	Beinn Eighe Nature Reserve West Ross-shire, Scotland (open heather grazing)
Birds	27%	8%
Mammals	17%	38%
Frogs and lizards	2%	0%
Fish	0%	1%
Invertebrates	31%	24%
Apples, berries and nuts	23%	29%

Surplus killing — what goes wrong?

A study of a black-headed gull colony in the north of England showed that hundreds of gulls were killed every breeding season by foxes, yet only about 3 per cent were eaten. The killing occurred on dark rainy nights when the gulls could simply be taken from the nests and made little or no attempt to escape. Such 'surplus killing' is not good for the prey, obviously, nor is it good for the predator, as it is wasteful of prey and could well wipe them out. Yet it happens — stoats and weasels will surplus kill confined birds; rats will do so with confined mice; wolves will do so with domestic stock; it has even been recorded that polar bears will kill, and not eat, ice-trapped narwhals. The natural methods of escape of the prey in such cases do not help them escape, because they are confined, and the predator is over-stimulated by such unnaturally easy prey. Even though they have fed, and will therefore stop searching and hunting prey, the predators, when presented with so much plenty, may not stop catching and killing. Happily, it is rare in nature, but, by confining suitable prey, man increases the probability of it occurring.

THE TRUTH BEHIND MASS KILLINGS

Predators

The size of small mustelids, particularly the smaller weasels and stoats, means that they are fair game for most bigger predators. The traditional, rather naive, notion of chivalry between predators, a sort of honour among thieves that prevents them killing each other, is nonsense.

Dogs, cats, foxes and other large mammalian predators can and do kill weasels and stoats. However, because of their smelly anal scent glands, weasels and stoats are not very appetizing and hence, though they are

killed by larger mammals, they are not often eaten by them. Large wild carnivores will commonly kill small mustelids; it has even been suggested that foxes in parts of North America control populations of small mustelids. Otters and martens have been reported eating and possibly killing stoats. Domestic cats commonly kill but do not eat weasels and stoats. A Mammal Society survey in Britain of 'What the cat brought in' during 1979/80 recorded seven weasels and three stoats. It is probable that if there were fewer or no dogs and cats around human habitations people would see more small mustelids. Indeed, our stone age ancestors, because they had no cats, were probably much more familiar with small mustelids than we are today. They would have welcomed their presence, as they would have preyed upon rodent pests. Dogs will even attack polecats and martens, tending to go for young or old animals.

However, probably much more important than mammalian predators are birds of prey. Owls, falcons, eagles, even crows, gulls and herons, have been recorded as predators of small mustelids. Birds cannot smell, so have no inhibitions about eating smelly small mustelids. There are very few European birds of prey that have not had small mustelids, usually weasels, recorded in studies of their diets. For example, there are many recorded instances of kestrels attacking weasels and stoats. Occasionally, the weasel or stoat has been recorded to bite the kestrel and turn the tables, sometimes dramatically in mid-air.

As they are the commonest, weasels are the most frequent small mustelid recorded in the diets of birds of prey. However, it is known that stoats use their black-tipped tail to avoid such predators (see p. 21), which indicates that the danger is important to them.

An American scientist showed how this works very elegantly. He built a series of false animals out of foam and fur, with a black area in various places, including the tail, and sometimes with no black area or tail at all. Then on the roof of the lion house at Chicago Zoo he put these models in turn on a pulley at ground level. Moving the models across the flat roof he flew falcons at them and recorded the number of misses and 'kills' (see drawing). Those without the black-tipped tail were 'killed' more often than those with such tails. The stoat (and weasel) models were missed most frequently. The falcons were observed grasping at the black-tipped tails, which, due to their lack of dexterity and the thinness of the tail, they usually missed. It was clear that weasels with short tails and stoats with black-tipped tails were the best adapted of the models.

However, birds of prey do not confine themselves to the smaller mustelids. There are records of golden eagles taking martens and polecats

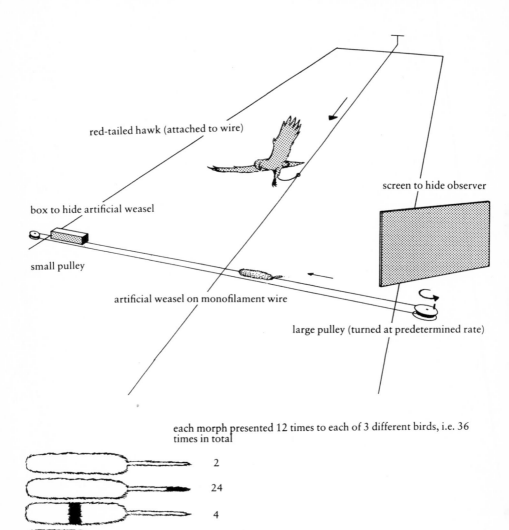

red-tailed hawk (attached to wire)

screen to hide observer

box to hide artificial weasel

small pulley

artificial weasel on monofilament wire

large pulley (turned at predetermined rate)

each morph presented 12 times to each of 3 different birds, i.e. 36 times in total

2

24

4

25

2

3

numbers = number of times a bird missed, i.e. proves stoat and weasel are best adapted versions

The Chicago Lion House experiment (see text).

from mainland Europe. It may be a surprise to some that golden eagles would take such large prey, but they have been known to attack even larger prey, such as the young of red deer and even badgers. Recently golden eagles turned up to nest in England and reared a single young bird. Among the prey brought to this fledgling were four stoats.

The ever-present danger represented by birds of prey is a likely explanation of the reported reluctance of small mustelids, in particular stoats and martens, to move out of cover. Indeed all small mustelids tend to move very rapidly, often zig-zagging when on clear ground, probably for the same reason. Predation by birds may also influence their activity patterns; for example, it has been suggested that in Wytham Wood (see pp. 18 and 19) weasels are active by day to avoid night active tawny owls.

Man is also an important predator, particularly in Britain. Whereas this has little influence on the populations of stoats and weasels which quickly replace those killed, it has had dramatic effects on the slower breeding martens and polecats.

Parasites

Stoats and weasels regularly have fleas in their fur. In very cold areas, such as Scandinavia, these fleas will be specific (i.e. they only live on stoats and weasels), but in milder climates such as Britain they are always fleas that properly belong on other animals, and none are specific. It is likely that this is because in colder areas, stoats and weasels are more dependent on their own nests for warmth, whereas in milder areas they can simply take over another animal's nest and hence also acquire that animal's fleas. Some investigators have suggested that the fleas found on stoats and weasels could indicate what animals they are eating. However, detailed analysis of flea species found on stoats, weasels and martens has shown that they principally acquire fleas from temporarily occupied dens (see Denning).

Ticks are also found on small mustelids, usually around the ears and shoulders. These are usually the so-called hedgehog ticks *Ixodes hexagonus* (see drawing) which could in truth be equally well called the mustelid tick. Lice, which are tiny little insects, are also found on small mustelids. Martens, stoats and weasels have their own type of louse. They are most commonly found on the animal's underside, around the groin and also on the head.

Mites, which, like ticks, are not insects but relatives of spiders, can also be found in the fur of small mustelids and their prey. However, the most bizarre aspect of parasitic mites concerns a type of mite that looks somewhat like a little crocodile, called *Demodex*. It is found in the hair follicles of rodents and other mammals. These mites, because they occur so deep in the skin, are virtually impossible to find except by destroying the skin. However, recently a German investigator found such mites from a rodent prey in a weasel's droppings, which is strange, since digestion usually destroys all mites. So if you want to find these mites, have a look at some droppings.

The most disturbing parasite found in small mustelids is a nematode worm which has the remarkable name of *Skrjabingylus nasicola*. The adult stage of this worm lives in the animal's cranium and can damage the skull, actually causing holes to appear (see drawing). It is not known how these affect the victims. It was thought that these worms were picked up only from shrews, but then the worms were found in New Zealand stoats; as there are no shrews in New Zealand, this disproved that idea.

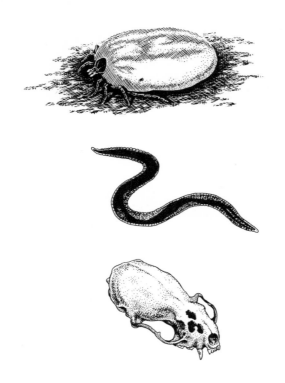

(Top) *Tick,* (middle) *skull nematode and* (below) *skull damage by nematode.*

These parasitic worms are common. Between 20-50 per cent of European stoats and weasels suffer from worm-damaged skulls and a higher percentage may actually be infested. Such damage is less common in polecats and martens, possibly because they have thicker skulls. The rate of damage to the skulls varies from place to place and this has been linked to rainfall. Dampness is likely to be important to the young stages of the worm.

All in all, a rather nasty collection of parasites. However, most animals naturally carry some parasites, so it is not at all unusual. It is important to remember, however, that these parasites do cost their hosts something and that they are likely to influence their behaviour. For example, a build-up of ectoparasites in nest material in the den is one of the likely reasons for frequent den changes by small mustelids and the airing of nest material by polecats (see Denning).

Martens, polecats and plague

As small mustelids move over relatively large areas they may be responsible for spreading disease from place to place. This is particularly true of flea-borne diseases, as they are frequently infested by other animals' fleas. Take, for example, bubonic plague: the fleas found on Californian martens in North America are often fleas from wild rodents, usually from chipmunks and ground squirrels. Both chipmunks and ground squirrels there suffer from bubonic plague. This disease is transmitted by fleas and it is not surprising therefore that the martens get plague. As rodents do not travel very far, but martens do, the martens may well be responsible for carrying plague from place to place. They may therefore play an important role in the ecology of plague in California.

Similarly in North-West China, plague is present in another rodent: the marmot. A Chinese scientist studying marmot fleas was surprised to discover that some of the fleas in his study area had travelled 470 metres (513 yards) in 14 days, quite a feat for a flea even on a marmot. He considered it likely that the fleas had hitched a ride on polecats to have made such a journey. As in California, the mobile small mustelid may play a role in the ecology of plague in certain areas of China. There is no plague in Britain today, so British martens and polecats are quite safe in this regard.

Signs

Small mustelids are rare and elusive in comparison with other mammals. Finding out if they are present and what they are doing therefore often requires looking at what they leave behind: tracks, scats (droppings), hair tufts and remains of kills. Such things are referred to as a sign, or spoor. Being able to find and understand such signs in the field is difficult and takes time to learn. Such sign-reading along with trapping is referred to as field craft, a sadly neglected subject among scientists. The lure of fancy gadgets, both in and outside the laboratory, has over-shadowed what is regarded by some as an outdated skill. However, for the full utilization of such recent techniques as radiotracking, such field craft is essential.

One of the most commonly found signs of small mustelids is their scats. The relative sizes and shapes of such scats are detailed in the diagram. Weasel scats can vary in shape and colour, depending on what they have

Scats (droppings) of British small mustelids

Shape & Size

Weasel	Long, thin and tapered. Approximately 3-6mm long and 2mm across.	
Stoat	Long, thin and coiled. Approximately 4-8mm long and 5mm across.	
Polecat	Long, thin and twisted. Up to 70mm long and 5-9mm across.	
Marten	Sausage shaped and often coiled. Approximately 40-120mm long and up to 12mm across.	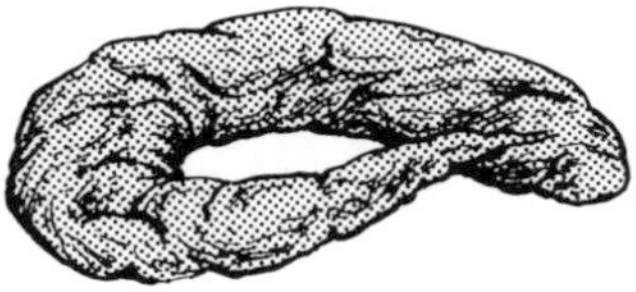

eaten. They usually contain hair, sometimes feathers and when fresh have a musky smell. They are long, often twisted and pointed at both ends. They can sometimes be found in large numbers in dens and are used to mark territories.

Stoat scats are similar in shape to those of weasels, but are often larger. They can also contain hair, feathers and sometimes bones. They smell musky when fresh, and are used as territorial markers. They also occur at dens, often in large numbers. Polecats' droppings vary a great deal according to diet and when fresh they smell unpleasant. If the polecat has been feeding on amphibians, the scats will be loose and fairly liquid. They are usually long, thin, tapered and sometimes coiled, composed of hair, feathers, bits of bone and insect remains. Despite their smell, they do not appear to be used as territorial markers (unlike weasel, stoat and marten scats). They are usually found in regular latrines near the den. Polecat scats are also found near the remains of prey.

Marten scats are, like those of polecats, highly variable. They are usually sausage-shaped and will often contain fruit and berry remains in autumn. They are normally dark, coiled and have a pleasant musty smell. They have been described as smelling like violets. Marten scats have been successfully used as indicators of marten presence during surveys of marten distribution. This is because they are easily found since they are deposited in obvious places such as on ant hills, rocks and logs as well as at the sides of regularly used marten paths.

It is very difficult to be absolutely sure of the identity of a small mustelid scat, as there is a great deal of variability in size, shape and colour. Only experience of seeing and smelling them will enable you to be confident in

Marten claw marks on a stone wall.

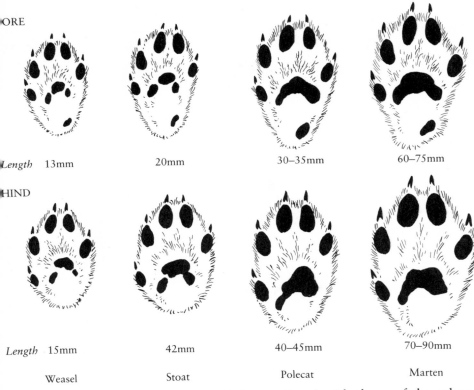

FORE

| Length | 13mm | 20mm | 30–35mm | 60–75mm |

HIND

| Length | 15mm | 42mm | 40–45mm | 70–90mm |

Weasel   Stoat   Polecat   Marten

identification. Mink scats can easily be confused with those of the other small mustelids, particularly polecats; one factor that can indicate a mink is if the scat contains lots of fish.

All small mustelids have five toes and a central pad or pads on both fore and hind feet. Their claws are non-retractable. For this reason, the tracks of small mustelids often show claw marks, unlike those of other mammals with retractable claws, such as cats. Indeed, where martens cross stones or rocks, one can often see scratches made by their claws (see drawing).

It is rare to find clear tracks of weasels; as they are so small and light, they will only leave marks on the softest snow or mud. If the weasel is moving quickly there may be a distance of up to 30 cm (12 inches) between groups of tracks.

Stoat tracks are usually bigger than weasels'. They are often in groups of two when you see a complete 'registration' (hind feet landing where forefeet were when the animal is moving at speed). There can be gaps of

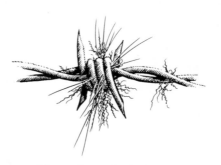

Marten fur on barbed wire.

up to 50 cm (20 inches) between the groups of tracks. As with weasels', stoat tracks are not seen often and are left only on soft mud, sand or snow. Tractor tracks are good places to look, as are stream and pond edges.

Polecat tracks are usually bigger than those of stoats, although stoats' hind feet can be as long as those of polecats (see diagram). The claw mark, if present, is likely to be long, blunt but very distinct. There can be up to 50 cm (20 inches) between groups of tracks, as with stoats.

Pine marten tracks radiate out which can distinguish them from other small mustelid tracks (see diagram). They are bigger than those of other small mustelids and look like cats' tracks, but the claws and number of toes distinguish them (cats have only four toes). There can be up to 90 cm (35½ inches) between groups of tracks. The tracks register if the animal is bounding, and then you find them in groups of two. Pine martens also tend to leave little clumps of hair on thorns, snags and barbed-wire fences. As their hair is very characteristic (see drawing), this can be a useful indicator of the user of a path.

Mink tracks are more splayed than those of martens and polecats. Also the mink's tail often leaves a mark called 'tail drag', which is unusual for martens and polecats. Watch out, for tracks vary a great deal. For example, one toe often may not show, which can be confusing. You will never find a perfect track, and it will NEVER look just like the illustration in a book (even this one!).

As there is such a difference between sizes of male and female small mustelids, it has occurred to some people that it might be possible to tell the sexes apart by the size of their tracks. This idea has been examined for American fishers, a species where the sexes are very different in size (see p. 53), and it was found that there were differences in the lengths of male and female tracks. But, because there was considerable overlapping of sexes, only about 15 per cent of fishers could be accurately sexed by their tracks. Such a method is even less likely to work for small mustelid species.

Any carcass, or remains of a carcass, of a small mammal, bird or rabbit, with bite-marks on the back of the neck or skull is likely to have been killed by a small mustelid. Some small mustelids will also chew the head and legs off birds. They sometimes kill birds by biting under the wing, which is very effective because there is a large number of blood vessels there.

(Top) *Feathers chewed by small mustelid and* (below) *rabbit with characteristic bite wound at the back of the neck.*

Polecats, and occasionally other small mustelids, eat the brains of their prey first. This also occurs when rodents kill and eat each other. Stoats sometimes lap blood from the bite wound, thereby giving rise to incorrect stories about stoats sucking blood from their prey. A very characteristic behaviour of small mustelids is cacheing (hiding) of prey (hiding prey by

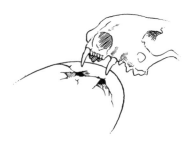

Bird's eggs attacked by small mustelids; note the signs of canine teeth marks and distance apart of teeth.

burying or covering with stones). If there is a surplus of prey that the animal cannot eat the extra will be cached. This behaviour has also been noted in foxes and other carnivores.

At birds' nests, small mustelids are considered to be relatively 'clean' predators, leaving the nest itself undisturbed; apart from broken eggshells, cached nestlings if they can be found or scats, there will be little evidence. The eggs, however, can be examined for teeth marks as the canine teeth of mustelids often leave distinct puncture holes in the shells (see drawing). The distance apart of the puncture holes can be measured and sometimes the species responsible identified. Puncture holes at a distance of between 5-14 mm are almost certainly those of small mustelids (including mink). In this range there is obviously a great deal of overlap between species of small mustelids. However, with knowledge of the local habitat, signs and careful measurements, it is often possible to identify the species of nest predator responsible.

Measuring the distance apart of puncture holes in other prey such as mammals and amphibians may also be worthwhile. For instance, polecats leave the heads of toads, probably because they contain poison glands. As polecats kill toads by a bite at the base of the head it is often possible to measure the distance between the tooth punctures of such remains.

Smells

Smells play an important role in the lives of most mammals. Unlike modern man, other mammals use smells a great deal to communicate. This is particularly true for all the weasel family and for most, if not all, carnivores. They live in a world where recognition of where you are (and who you are) is determined by smell.

Small mustelids produce smells from the secretions of their anal scent glands. These are the most obvious and probably the most important glands. However there are other scent glands. Neck glands have been identified in young mustelids by investigators in the Soviet Union and these may well be associated with the neck mane found on young stoats (see p. 60). Martens, stoats, weasels and polecats also rub their chins on objects in a manner which suggests they have chin glands. Curiously, the American fisher has areas of coarse hair on its hind feet which are also considered to be associated with scent glands.

Small mustelids will use scent for different purposes: if they are frightened, they will eject anal scent gland secretions, often at predators. This is obviously very distasteful to the predator and may put it off competely. Anal scent gland secretions also have a function as territorial markers, often on scats. This marking of territories by smelly scats is found in martens, stoats and weasels; polecats appear to mark territories with urine which may also be specially scented. Such scent-marking of territories is very common in wild carnivores having been noted in, for example, otters, badgers, hyenas, foxes, wolves and coyote.

Scent is also believed to be important for recognizing individuals and for publicizing status in the hierarchy. Dominant stoats, for example, scent mark more frequently than under-dog stoats, and it is understood that by smelling each other, stoats can assess each other's status. Aggression in male ferrets is partly determined by scent; if a male can smell his own scent (i.e. he is in his own territory) he will be more aggressive than if he smells another's scent.

Scent also plays a sexual role in small mustelids, although this is at present little understood. It is known that ferrets can distinguish between male and female smells. Hardly surprisingly, they were more attracted to the smell of the opposite sex! This also appears to be the case for stoats. For example, while trapping Irish stoats, I once baited traps with male stoat anal scent gland secretions and there caught only females.

Although scent has important functions for small mustelids, there are costs: firstly, the cost of producing the scent; also the disadvantage that prey, by smelling the mustelid, will get an early warning and attempt to avoid it. British investigators have shown that voles do just this innately when confronted by stoat or weasel scent. Curiously wood mice show no such response and this remains something of a mystery.

Scientific studies

Scientific research on small mustelids is done in two very different environments: the laboratory and the field. Each complements the other and frequently studies involve some work in both environments. Laboratory work can involve, for example, looking at captive animals' behaviour, physiology and genetics. Whole carcasses are also examined in the laboratory. Their overall body size and coat colour would be noted, then, depending on the aim of the study, a variety of other aspects can be investigated including parasites, gut contents, pesticide levels, even genetics. Generally, the coat is retained as a study skin and the skull or penile bone is treated and kept for further study.

Stoat and weasel carcasses for study are often acquired from gamekeepers, but it is also possible to use road casualties. The source of the carcasses can bias a study; for example, gamekeepers trap mainly males and usually at certain times of the year and road casualties are again seasonal and mainly males.

Laboratory work also includes looking for prey remains from scats and guts. These are then identified to build up a picture of the animal's diet. Identification involves using parts of prey to identify what was eaten: things like hairs, bones of mammals, feathers, beaks and claws of birds and, when they occur, amphibian, reptile, fish and invertebrate remains. The gut contents or scats are usually sieved, washed and cleaned before being sorted out and identified, usually under a microscope. In order to be confident of the identification a reference collection of these bits and pieces of typical prey needs to be available for comparison. A knowledge of the local habitat in which the animal was feeding is very useful, particularly in the analysis of pine marten dietary remains when all sorts of vegetable material is likely to turn up.

Library and museum research is another vital resource. Old references were, for example, used to reconstruct the history of the decline of polecats and martens in Britain. From this study came recommendations about protection of these species so that they could be assured a future. Many museums have collections of study skins, skulls and often stuffed small mustelids. These can be useful in the study of body size, coat colour and even damage by the nasty nematode skull parasite (see Parasites).

However, field studies offer a bigger challenge and only by such studies can small mustelids be fully understood. Such studies involve marking,

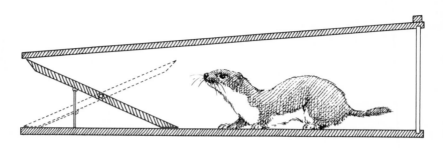

A stoat in a wooden 'continental' live trap.

live-trapping and re-trapping which yield information about the population density, home range, diet and behaviour. Trapping small mustelids is a tricky dangerous affair and should not be attempted by untrained individuals. It is also notoriously difficult and this is one of the reasons why these animals are so poorly understood. Weasels and stoats are usually 'live-trapped' (meaning that the animals are released after being examined) in wooden tunnel traps called 'continental' traps. These traps work by a see-saw arrangement where the animal's own weight sets off the trap (see drawing) — cunning, eh? Rabbit's guts, canned fishy cat food and anal scent gland secretions are among the baits used. The traps are equipped with non-absorbent bedding and some food, usually a dead white mouse. The bedding and the fact that the trap is made of wood, rather than metal, are both meant to keep the animal warm and dry until it is released. The traps are inspected twice a day so that the animals are confined for a maximum period of twelve hours, usually less. Stoats and weasels are easily chilled and will quickly die if cold in a damp, confined space. The food serves a double purpose, it keeps the animal going while it is in the trap, and stimulates the animal to produce scats. The scats can be collected from the trap and used for diet studies.

Weasels, being small, are particularly susceptible to cold in traps, so it is a good idea to close such traps at night during very cold weather. Weasels and even young or small stoats occasionally turn up in metal small mammal traps (called Longworth traps). In such conditions, they sometimes die. However, if they live and the unsuspecting researcher opens the trap, the trapper usually gets a very prompt bite for his or her troubles. Experienced small-mammal scientists are well aware of this (once bitten, twice shy) and they will gingerly sniff extra heavy traps for the give-away mustelid smell before opening them. Small mustelids are probably attracted to small mammal traps because they have mice or voles in them or simply because the entrance to the trap is a small hole, likely to be that of a small mammal. Martens and polecats are not as susceptible to cold and damp as weasels and stoats and are usually caught in wire traps. Once caught, the animals are anaesthetized before handling, often in specially designed boxes with windows to allow the animal's state to be observed during the procedure.

One of the great difficulties in field studies of small mustelid populations is that they are so widely spread out. This particularly applies to stoats and the larger small mustelids. Take stoats as an example: on average, an area of 30-40 hectares (74-100 acres) needs to be trapped to get one stoat. As at least, say, six stoats are needed for a respectable study, the area trapped needs to be at least 200 hectares (495 acres). This area needs to be traversed twice a day to check the traps, and there are frequently considerable distances involved.

When stoat trapping in Ireland, attempting to cover up to 316 hectares (780 acres) at Fota (see Stoats) I found myself walking up to 30 kilometres (18 miles) per day — and this was even with the aid of a van. Most of this was necessary because the habitat was inaccessible in a van, as small

STEVE, REMEMBER TO SMELL THE TRAP FOR WEASELS BEFORE OPENING IT.

mustelid habitats tend to be. To get around the problem one can get an extra person, but this adds considerably to the cost of the research. Alternatively, some researchers recommend using a horse or motor cycle, but even then it is difficult to manoeuvre (indeed very difficult to manoeuvre the former) into a position from where one can view each trap. The problem is serious enough for a stoat trapping system to have been specially designed to overcome it. In New Zealand, such a system exists with a mercury switch on the trap doors. The switch connects to an electrical flex which goes to a convenient check point, for example near a road, where by use of a special gadget the trapper can tell whether the trap has an inhabitant.

Tracking of small mustelids was in the past only possible in snow and therefore was confined to areas where there was lots of snow, like Finland and Russia. It could only be done in winter and involved skilled sign reading, and usually proficiency on skis. However, radiotracking, which involves fitting a tiny transmitter onto the animal, has superseded snow tracking. The radio-transmitter and attachment (called a radio-tag) are fitted around the animal's neck and studies are done on captive animals to ensure they do not cause the animal inconvenience or alter its behaviour.

When in operation, the radio-tag gives off a signal, usually a regular bleep, about 40-80 times a minute. The investigator uses a portable radio-receiver and an aerial to locate the animal (called, in jargon, 'taking a fix'). Sometimes, semi-permanent receivers and aerials are left in the field with specially attached tape recorders so that the investigators can get some sleep! Eventually either the tag falls off or the animal is re-trapped and the tag removed.

Stoat wearing radio tag.

Using radiotracking means that the animal can be located and sometimes observed. However, small mustelids, particularly stoats and martens, have proved very difficult to see in the field, even when you know where they should be. This is due to their deft use of cover. Understandably radiotracking has revolutionized the study of many mammals, including small mustelids and many other carnivores.

Radiotracking can lead the observer into some very odd situations; everybody has his or her own radiotracking funny story. The tracker has a radio receiver, a large aerial (like a TV aerial), usually ear phones, a notebook and other equipment. Consequently, one gets strange looks. People I met while radiotracking Irish stoats would often begin to comb their hair and smarten their appearance. It took me some time to realize what prompted this behaviour, but in the end I found out that many of them thought they were about to be on TV!

So what research can someone without a laboratory or radio-tags do? The most basic, yet important, scientific information about an animal is its distribution — where it occurs both in terms of the country as a whole and in terms of local habitats. In Britain and Ireland, we know where small mustelids occur geographically, although there are undoubted gaps which could be filled in the distribution maps. However, the localized habitat preferences (see pp. 41 and 42) have received little attention and would be a very rewarding area for further study. Records of sightings and road casualty casualty records of small mustelids could provide useful data on such local habitat preferences. Such records could be sent to your local mammal group or county naturalists' trust.

Energetics

All animals need energy to live. All actions require energy: even if the animal does nothing, it needs energy to keep its body ticking over. The scientific study of the role of energy in living things is called ecological energetics. It can be approached at two levels. Firstly, the energetics of an individual animal can be studied. Alternatively, the energetics of populations of animals within communities, which will describe energy flow through such communities, can be examined.

An example of the first approach is some work done on fishers in the United States. The first study of the energetics of any free living wild carnivore was done on fishers in the forests of Michigan. To begin with two tame fishers were trained to run on a laboratory treadmill which allowed basic fisher energy requirements and utilization to be measured. Then the fisher's energetics was tested in the field by radiotracking wild fishers.

The wild fishers were found to move more slowly and sleep a great deal more than the fishers in the laboratory, hence they needed less energy. While being radiotracked, they killed porcupines, hares, squirrels and mice and also ate carrion. When the calculations were complete it was found that the free-living fishers were acquiring more energy per day from their diet than they needed. Indeed almost all the wild fishers radiotracked reflected this by being very healthy and well padded with fat. No wonder they slept a great deal.

These results and the marked sexual dimorphism in fishers (see Ecological roles) were interpreted as a possible explanation for the small size of females: that being smaller, they have lower energy demands while rearing young. The males in Michigan were bigger than males elsewhere in the United States, but the females were about the same size. If there is all this surplus food/energy around, why did the females not get bigger if small size did not confer an adaptive advantage on them? As we have seen (Growing up), rearing young is difficult for female mustelids and must cost them a great deal of energy. However, the difference in size of the sexes is mainly determined in the nest and early growing stage and may well be linked to early reproductive development in females.

In communities of mammal prey, predation can have an impact if the prey are at a low density but at high densities predation appears often to have little impact on prey numbers. The consumption of small mammals by weasels has been measured; in an old field in Michigan, weasels consumed 31 per cent of the yearly production of meadow mice. However, the mice only consumed 2 per cent of the available vegetable food. Many mice came into the field from outside, thereby providing the weasels with additional prey. In the Wytham Wood study (see pp. 18-19), weasels consumed 14 per cent of the small mammals per year.

All organic matter, including energy, is produced by green plants. Some of this energy is used by herbivores and then in turn by carnivores. Each time the energy is used by an animal a staggering 98 per cent of it is lost as it is used in maintenance and not growth or reproduction. The loss of such a great deal of energy means that the flow of energy through communities is very inefficient and fewer and fewer animals can exist the further you get away from green plants. This is why, in energetic terms, small mustelids are relatively rare (see p. 13). The study of energetics in small mustelids, particularly of free-living small mustelids, is likely to provide important information about their biology and how they take part in energy flow through communities.

Captive and tame small mustelids

This topic is difficult because each small mustelid is an individual, with his or her own character, just like other animals (and people). This is well known to anyone who has radiotracked wild small mustelids or managed to tame one. Bearing this in mind some generalizations can be made.

Captivity suits some small mustelids and not others, and it suits some species more than others. Polecats, if taken young enough, will thrive in captivity, hence they are by far the most common species of small mustelid in captivity. Martens on the other hand are very shy and extremely difficult to get to breed in captivity. Stoats and weasels will adapt to captivity and, like polecats, will take to it better the younger they are taken. However, they are both jumpy and short-lived, so it is difficult to maintain a captive colony.

Keeping carnivores in captivity, even such small carnivores, is very unnatural, as they are adapted to ranging over large areas. Compare some of the ranges mentioned in this book to the size of a zoo cage and you will appreciate this. Hence when in captivity certain carnivores including small mustelids are prone to display unnatural behaviour such as eating their own young and possible sexual maladjustment (see Breeding).

Some species will become tame in captivity, others will become tame in the wild — or at least become less wild. Polecats, particularly if crossed with ferrets and handled regularly, will become very tame in captivity but in the wild they are not reported to lose their instinctive fear of man.

Wild martens on the other hand are reported in Scotland to regularly take food, usually sandwiches and biscuits, from forestry workers. They also visit bird tables and have even been known to enter an occupied house to procure food. It is important to note the family who live in this house do not have a dog. Curiously such behaviour is not reported from the few remaining populations of martens in England. It may be that the Scottish race is uniquely friendly.

The ancient Greeks and Romans are said to have kept tame martens to control rodents, before the domestic cat came along. Because of this it is said that they introduced martens to various islands in the Mediterranean. However, do not be tempted to follow their example, as confining wild

martens is now illegal in Britain and Ireland and should not be attempted.

People have tried to tame stoats and weasels with varying degrees of success. Wild adult animals will not become tame, but there is some chance of young ones doing so. In the last century a Captain Lyon of the Royal Navy took a stoat to sea in order to tame it, but the stoat died at sea. It regularly bit Captain Lyon before it died, as all mustelids, no matter how tame, will do from time to time. A French lady, Mademoiselle de Laistre, kept a weasel in a cage in her bedroom. She would allow it out to sleep in her quilt and it was said to be most affectionate. Apparently she disguised its smell with perfume.

More recently, an Australian racing driver, Peter Harris, on a visit to Britain, found a very young weasel and tamed it very successfully. It loved to be stroked and to have its ears rubbed and used to get up to all kinds of antics. He called it Teasey and when he returned to Australia he gave it to the author Phil Drabble, who wrote about it (and other tame animals) in his book *A Weasel in My Meatsafe* (see References).

In all your dealings with small mustelids remember they *bite*, and will bite even if they are tame. Should you want to keep wild small mustelids, remember they will need a variety of good quality food, such as eggs, meat or pet food. The variety is important, as captive small mustelids, once they are used to one kind of food, will not readily take to another. They will

also need spacious and very secure hutches with warm and dry nesting areas. A good start should you wish to keep captive small mustelids is to keep ferrets, and there are many good books on keeping ferrets (see References).

A few other hints, should you come across lost, injured or diseased small mustelids: ferrets are the only ones you'll find lost, as they quite often are. Should you find one you should try to find its owner or else contact a local ferreting society. Injured or diseased wild small mustelids are sometimes found. Remember they will bite, so think twice before you handle them. You should take them to a veterinary surgeon and in the case of martens you should report them to the Nature Conservancy Council or wildlife office.

Folklore

All over the world there are traditional beliefs about small mustelids. Some of these have at least a grain of truth in them, others are based on accurate, if misinterpreted, observations. For example, there are folktales among Europeans, Chinese and North American Indians explaining why the stoat's tail tip is black. For example, the stoat blackened its tail in a fire or was given the black tail by a god or goddess, as an identifying mark. Clearly the black tail's distinctiveness was widely recognized and people felt it needed explaining, as do scientists today (see p. 77). There is a widespread, completely unfounded, story about martens like other carnivores (lions for instance) having hooks or claws in their tails with which they can do great destruction. This story has no basis in fact.

Across Britain there are tales about ghostly white weasels which are often said to be harbingers of disaster or death or even to be evil spirits. These ghostly white weasels were very likely stoats that had gone white in winter. Such stoats do look very odd and ghostly, particularly if there is no snow about.

Other folktales and children's stories simply reflect superstitions or prejudices without any basis in fact or accurate observations; small mustelids, particularly weasels, stoats and ferrets, have a poor image. For example, there are widespread stories in Britain telling of the bad luck that will befall you should a weasel cross your path, particularly, so it is said, at the start of a journey. This bad luck very much depends on which way the weasel turns off the path, but this varies according to where the tale is told. In Wales, on the other hand, a traditional belief has it that if a weasel goes before you without turning back you will win something.

The Irish are equally superstitious about weasels (as stoats are called in Ireland — see p. 16) but often show a grudging respect. Country people believe that bad luck will visit anyone who interferes with a weasel's nest or kills a weasel. The weasels' relatives will take revenge, poisoning milk by spitting in it or simply following the guilty person and relentlessly dogging them for the rest of their days. There is a story of an Irish emigrant going to America and being followed by a vengeful 'weasel'.

These tales may have a lot to do with the fearlessness of small mustelids and the fact that they will stay around and look at people, unlike other wild animals. There is no need for us to fear such behaviour or invent tales to explain it; sadly, children's stories in Britain are often prejudiced against small mustelids. For example, in *Wind in the Willows* armed stoats and weasels from the wild wood invade and occupy Toad Hall, a stately home. The stoats and weasels are characterized as cowardly, bullying and unpleasant creatures, the villains of the book. In another children's book *Nicholas Thomas gets into Trouble* a stoat family, described as rough, ragged rogues, attempts to trick Nicholas Thomas (a young cat) in order to cook and eat him. Perhaps the most amusing reference is in *Winnie the Pooh*. Pooh tracks a 'woozle' in the snow around a tree only to find that the number of woozles increases each time he rounds the tree! The woozle is a creature enormously feared by Pooh and Piglet, being described as possibly of 'hostile intent'.

What does all this mean? I reckon it is a prejudice based on the fact that small mustelids were considered common vermin by the upper class, who were interested in game preservation. It is perhaps no accident that the stoats and weasels are described in two of the books as being common, or lower class. One of the dangers of anthropomorphism. It is high time small mustelids got a better, more accurate image, particularly in children's books.

Mankind also has widespread folklore about small mustelid products. For example, a purse made out of a piebald weasel skin in Ireland is considered to be very lucky. Ermine fur is still used by royalty (see p. 49) and was also used to adorn North American Indian head-dresses. Black-footed ferret skins appear in the past to have had a mystic significance for many tribes of North American Indians including the Sioux, Blackfoot, Crow, Cheyenne and Pawnee. It is likely that the Indians were aware of the species' rarity, even then, and hence valued it highly. The skins were used by them as pendants on head-dresses or in sacred tobacco and other ceremonies.

Conservation

Some small mustelids may themselves be in need of conservation; though they are also occasionally considered to be responsible for threatening the existence of other species, in particular endangered birds. The most important example of this is that of introduced stoats and other small mustelids endangering New Zealand's native birds.

New Zealand is made up of two large remote islands where the fauna evolved separately from the rest of the world. There were few mammals. When the first people (Maori) arrived, there were only two native mammals, both of which were bats. All sorts of different native birds had evolved to fill the mammal roles in the available habitats. Due to the absence of predators, the birds were often flightless and had no fear of mammals. They were therefore particularly vulnerable. The most celebrated example of these birds is the kiwi, symbol of New Zealand, but there are many more.

When man, both Maori and European, introduced dogs, cats, rats, pigs and small mustelids to New Zealand the devastating effect on the native birds was quickly apparent. Indeed on many of the world's remote islands, similar introductions have destroyed native island faunas. In New Zealand stoats are seen as a major threat to native birds, and there is little doubt that they can and do prey on the native birds. Because of this there have been bloodthirsty calls for widespread stoat control there.

Painstaking work on stoats and native birds by scientists in New Zealand has shown that the effect of such stoat control is questionable, as it is on British game estates. Some of New Zealand's birds are already extinct or close to extinction. The major threat to them is habitat destruction, so vigorous habitat protection would be the best way of saving them, particularly on islands (see pp. 42 and 43), backed up perhaps by limited predator control when absolutely necessary.

An interesting example is that of the takahe, a heavily built, long-lived, flightless native New Zealand bird. It was once found all over New Zealand, but was considered to be extinct by 1898. Then, happily, a small population was found on the South Island in 1948. However, despite being protected, the population did not increase as expected and stoats appeared to be to blame. There had been good mouse years in the area and for this reason stoats were sometimes very common.

However, research in the 1970s by the New Zealand Wildlife Service

Takahe – a flightless native New Zealand bird supposedly threatened by stoats.

quickly identified another introduced mammal that was causing the takahe much more serious problems than stoats. Surprisingly it was red deer, which were common in the area. Both the takahe and the deer liked to graze the same sort of tussock plants. The deer were grazing this tussock so hard that there was little available for the takahe. Consequently it was the control of deer and not stoats that became the main management priority for the Wildlife Service in the takahe area.

As small mustelids themselves are elusive and not easily found, it is often difficult to determine if they themselves are in need of conservation measures or not. Many, such as stoats and weasels in Britain, are still common and therefore have little need for conservation. However others, particularly the larger fur-bearers in northern countries, have declined and in some areas are endangered. Apart from these, there are also some small mustelids in various countries which may be endangered, but as yet there is so little known about them that this question is still open.

In Europe there is no doubt that the fur-bearers — the sable and marbled polecat — are indeed endangered. In North America it is now reasonably certain that the black-footed ferret is extinct in the wild and is clinging to survival as a captive species (see below). In Britain polecats and martens have become rare due to habitat destruction and relentless persecution by gamekeepers (see p. 49). Indeed, over much of their range, like many wild carnivores, the martens, polecats and their relatives are declining and are in need of conservation. Elsewhere the Siberian weasel, Malaysian weasel and the black-striped weasel of South East Asia are considered to be endangered but with so little known about them it is difficult to be sure. The water weasel, discovered in Colombia in 1978, again may be endangered but without further information little can be done about this species.

So what can be done to conserve these animals? Firstly, the status of each species, if unknown, has to be investigated to find out just how many of them there were and are, where they are and what habitats they prefer. Should it be established that the species is declining, a captive breeding programme should begin immediately before the animal becomes rare. Taking scarce wild animals from small populations for captive breeding can and has further threatened some species and should be avoided, if possible.

There are those that argue against captive breeding by claiming, possibly quite correctly, that once in captivity an animal ceases to be 'wild'. Captive breeding is also expensive and does tend to divert funds from other important conservation areas such as habitat protection and field studies. However, there are now sufficient examples of captive breeding giving species breathing space and leading to successful re-introductions to the wild that such arguments can be countered. Sadly there are few if any examples of small carnivores being successfully captive bred and re-introduced. It has been successful with other species, such as American bison, Hawaiian geese, oryx and whooping cranes, to name but a few, so it could work for small mustelids.

One of the most important aspects about re-introduction is that the factors that caused the animal to decline and become rare in the first place must be identified and rectified — otherwise the re-introduced animals will not survive. There are many factors that cause declines in small mustelids, such as direct persecution by man and habitat destruction. It is possible to legally protect threatened animals which should prevent human persecution and it is sometimes possible to preserve or reconstruct suitable habitat.

In the modern world there are other more recent dangers that are more difficult to control. The numbers of cars and lorries on our roads grows every year and so do the numbers of road casualty wild mammals. This is an ever-present danger to small mustelids, particularly in the breeding season. Also there are various poisons that can directly or indirectly threaten small mustelids; insecticides can build up in the tissues of predators and these ought to be monitored and controlled, if necessary. Sheep farmers leave carcasses poisoned by strychnine and other such poisons as a lure to kill dogs and foxes; these also kill carrion-eating small mustelids such as polecats and martens. This is considered to be a factor in the failure of Irish martens to spread in recent years. Such poisoning is indiscriminate and threatens many wild animals and domestic pets; it should be stopped in favour of more discriminating control techniques.

There are also the poisons (called anticoagulants) used to control rats, squirrels and mice that are necessary but may threaten small mustelids by secondary poisoning; if they eat poisoned rodents, they will ingest sufficient poison to kill themselves. Recent research in Denmark on beech martens suggests that the risk of secondary poisoning to them is slight. However, British research on polecats and weasels suggests they may sometimes be at risk.

What can the average reader do to help small mustelids? Keeping your domestic dogs and cats under control or indeed not having any at all, will help small mustelids. Using pesticides with care, particularly outdoor rat poisons, is another good idea. Encouraging legal protection and preserving habitats are also activities that can be assisted by joining one of the many conservation societies.

Small mustelids are residents of this planet just like us. They have a right to be here, and should be protected whenever practical and possible.

Will the black-footed ferret survive?

The black-footed ferret is a close relative of the polecat only found in North America. Unsurprisingly it has black legs and feet and looks rather like a polecat (see drawing). Its main prey was the prairie-dog, a burrowing member of the squirrel family. Prairie-dogs are pests of agriculture, so they were poisoned; their habitat was altered to suit modern farming. Numbers of prairie-dogs were reduced — but not as disastrously as numbers of black-footed ferrets. As predators, they were precariously less common than their prey species.

The effect of the prairie-dog decline on black-footed ferrets was so marked that they were considered rare by 1970 and extinct by 1980. Then one was killed by a dog near Meeteese, in Wyoming in 1981, thereby bringing attention to probably the last surviving wild population. It was established that some 60 or more ferrets were

Black-footed ferret in native habitat – sadly, probably now a thing of the past.

present in the area and this number increased to 128 animals by 1984. The black-footed ferret's future appeared secure. However disaster struck in 1985. The wild ferrets of Meeteese contracted a disease, canine distemper, which is fatal. All but 6 died and these survivors were taken into captivity. The black-footed ferret as a wild animal has become extinct, wiped out primarily by man and finally by a disease.

At the time of writing (1988) the captive ferrets are breeding well and there are now 40 or so. The colony has been split into three so that if some unforeseen tragedy occurs, it will probably not destroy the entire population. It is hoped that there will be sufficient ferrets to re-introduce some to the wild by 1991. However, at present with numbers so low, the survival of this small mustelid is in doubt.

Useful addresses

The Mammal Society
Baltic Exchange Building
21 Bury Street
London EC3A 5AU

Nature Conservancy Council
Northminster House
Peterborough PE1 1UA

National Ferret Welfare Society
Meadow View
Pheasants Hill
Hambleden
Henley-on-Thames
Oxon RG9 6SN

The Fauna and Flora Preservation Society
79-83 North Street
Brighton
East Sussex BN1 1ZA

References

It is not usual, in this type of book, to give a detailed reference list. However, there are few, if any popular books on small mustelids and the important references on small mustelids are difficult to find so I have included a brief reference list here. These references refer to subjects directly mentioned in the text or else are of more general interest. It is hoped that these will be of some assistance to those readers who wish to learn more about small mustelids.

Alcock, I. and P. Warsop, 'Diet, distribution and habitat preferences of stoats and weasels in Sheffield', *The Sorby Record, No. 20*: 5-10 (1982).

Blandford, P.R.S., 'Biology of the polecat *Mustela putorius*: a literature review', *Mammal Review 17*: 155-198 (1987).

Brodie, J., 'Mammalian predation on Norway rats *(Ratus norvegicus)* living in a rural environment' *Journal of Zoology*, London 216: 582-583 (1988).

Buchanan, J. B., 'Seasonality in the occurrence of long-tailed weasel road kills', *The Murrelet 68*: 67-68 (1987).

Burton, J. A. and B. Pearson, *Collins Guide to the rare mammals of the world* (Collins, London, 1987).

Buskirk, S. W., 'Seasonal use of resting sites by marten in South Central Alaska', *Journal of Wildlife Management 48*: 950-953 (1984).

Corbet, G. B. and H. N. Southern, *The Handbook of British Mammals* (Blackwells, Oxford, 1977).

Dagg, A. I., 'Homosexual behaviour and female male mounting in mammals', *Mammal Review 14*: 155-185 (1984).

Debrot, S. and C. Mermod, 'The spatial and temporal distribution pattern of the stoat *(Mustela erminea* L.)', *Oecologia* (Berlin) 59: 69-73 (1983).

Delany, M. J., *Mammal Ecology* (Blackie, London, 1982).

Drabble, P., *A Weasel in my Meatsafe* (Collins, London, 1957).

Erlinge, S., 'Spacing strategy in stoat *Mustela erminea*', *Oikos 28*: 32-42 (1977).

Erlinge, S., 'Agnostic behaviour and dominance in stoats *(Mustela erminea* L.)', *Z. Tierpsychol. 44*: 375-388 (1977).

Erlinge, S., M. Sandell and C. Brink, 'Scent-marking and its territorial significance in stoats, *Mustela erminea*', *Animal Behaviour 30*: 811-818 (1982).

Fairley, J. S., *An Irish Beast Book* (Blackstaff, Belfast, 1984).

Gorman, M. L., 'The response of prey to stoats (*Mustela erminea*) scent', *Journal of Zoology*, London *202*: 419-423 (1984).

Green, R. E., J. Howell and T. H. Johnson, 'Identification of predators of wader eggs from egg remains', *Bird Study 34*: 87-91 (1987).

Hansson, I., 'Cranial helmith parasites in species in Mustelidae', *Arkiv for Zoologi 22*: 571-594 (1970).

King, C. M., 'The weasel *Mustela nivalis* and its prey in an English woodland', *Journal of Animal Ecology 49*: 127-159 (1980).

King, C. M., *Immigrant Killers — Introduced Predators and the Conservation of Birds in New Zealand* (Oxford University Press, Auckland, 1984).

King, C. M. and R. L. Edgar, 'Techniques for trapping and tracking stoats *Mustela erminea*; a review and a new system', *New Zealand Journal of Zoology 4*: 193-212 (1977).

King, C. M. and P. J. Moors, 'On co-existence foraging strategy and biogeography of weasels and stoats *Mustela nivalis* and *M. erminea* in Britain', *Oecologia* (Berlin) *39*: 129-150 (1979).

King, C. M. and P. J. Moors, 'The life-history tactics of mustelids and their significance for predator control and conservation in New Zealand', *New Zealand Journal of Zoology 6*: 619-622 (1979).

King, C. M. and C. D. McMillan, 'Population structure and dispersal of peak-year cohorts of stoats (*Mustela erminea*) in two New Zealand forests with special reference to control', *New Zealand Journal of Ecology 5*: 59-66 (1982).

King, C. M. and J. E. Moody, 'The biology of the stoat (*Mustela erminea*) in the National Parks of New Zealand', *New Zealand Journal of Zoology 9*: 49-144 (1982).

Kruuk, H., 'Surplus killing by carnivores', *Journal of Zoology*, London, *166*: 233-244 (1972).

Langley, P. J. W. and D. W. Yalden, 'The decline of the rarer carnivores in Great Britain during the nineteenth century', *Mammal Review 7*: 95-116 (1977).

Lockie, J. D., 'The food of the pine-marten *Martes martes* in West Ross-shire, Scotland', *Proceedings of the Zoology Society of London 136*: 187-195 (1961).

Lockie, J. D., 'Territory in small carnivores', *Symposium of the Zoological Society of London 18*: 143-165 (1966).

Lockie, J. D., 'Studying carnivores', *Mammal Review 7*: 3-5 (1977).

Loos-Frank, B., 'The weasel (*Mustela nivalis*) helps in detecting *Demodex* mites in rodents', *Experimental and Applied Acarylogy* 4: 179-180 (1988).

Lund, M. and A. M. Rasmussen, 'Secondary poisoning hazards to stone martens *(Martes fonia)* fed bromadiolone-poisoned mice', *Nord. Vet-Med* 38: 241-243 (1986).

May, R. M., 'The cautionary tale of the black-footed ferret', *Nature 320*: 13-14 (1986).

McInerney, M., *A Taxonomic Study of some Western European Mustelids* (Unpublished B.Sc. Honours thesis, University College, Cork, Ireland, 1986).

Moors, P. J., 'Predation by mustelids and rodents on the eggs and chicks of native and introduced birds in Kourhai Bush, New Zealand', *Ibis 125*: 137-154 (1983).

Morris, R. B., 'Stoat predation at a red-billed gull colony, Kaikoura,' *Notomis 23*: 354-357 (1976).

Polder, E., 'Spotted skunk and weasel populations den and cover usage by Northeast Iowa', *Iowa Acad. Sci. 75*: 142-146 (1968).

Powell, R. A., *The Fisher* (University of Minnesota Press, Minneapolis, 1982).

Powell, R. A., 'Evolution of black-tipped tails in weasels: predator confusion', *The American Naturalist 119*: 126-131 (1982).

Pulliainen, E., 'Use of the home range by pine martens *(Martes martes* L.)', *Acta Zool. Fennica. 171*: 271-274 (1984).

Selwyn, S., 'Kestrel catching weasel', *British Birds 59*: 39 (1966).

Seton, E. T., *Lives of Game Animals* (Charles T. Branford, Boston, 1953).

Sgeulaiche, 'Puss, butch and peanut willie' (about tame wild martens) *B.B.C. Wildlife*, March 1988, pp. 134-137.

Simms, D. A., 'North American weasels: resource utilisation and distribution', *Canadian Journal of Zoology 57*: 504-520 (1979).

Sleeman, D. P., *The Ecology of the Irish Stoat* (Unpublished Ph.D. thesis, National University of Ireland, 1987).

Sleeman, D. P., '*Skrjabinbylus nasicola* (Leuckart) as a parasite of the Irish Stoat', *Irish Naturalist's Journal 22*: 525-527 (1988).

Sleeman, D. P., 'Irish stoat road casualties', *Irish Naturalist's Journal 22*: 527-529 (1988).

Smith, G. N., *Ferreting and Trapping* (Nimrod, Hants, 1979).

Spencer, W. D. and W. J. Zielinski, 'Predatory behaviour of pine martens', *Journal of Mammalogy 64*: 715-717 (1983).

Stoddart, D. M., 'Effect of the odour of weasels *(Mustela nivalis* L.) on trapped samples of their prey', *Oecologia 22*: 439-441 (1976).

Stuttard, R. M. (Ed.), *Predatory mammals in Britain — a code of practice for their management* (British Field Sports Society, London, 1986).

Tapper, S. C., R. E. Green and M. R. W. Rands, 'Effects of mammalian predators on partridge populations', *Mammal Review 12*: 156-167 (1982).

Taylor, R. H. and J. A. V. Tilley, 'Stoats *(Mustela erminea)* on Adele and Fisherman Islands, Abel Tasman National Park and other offshore islands in New Zealand', *New Zealand Journal of Ecology 7*: 139-145 (1984).

T.J.W., 'Weasel folklore in Munster', *Journal of the Royal Society of Antiquaries of Ireland 26*: 256-257 (1896).

Townsend, M. G., P. J. Bunyan, E. M. Odam, P. I. Stanley and H. P. Wardell, 'Assessment of secondary poisoning hazard of warfarin to least weasels', *Journal of Wildlife Management 48*: 628-632 (1984).

Velander, K. A., *Pine marten survey of Scotland, England and Wales 1980-1982* (Vincent Wildlife Trust, London, 1983).

Walker, D. G., 'The behaviour and movements of a juvenile golden eagle *Aquila chrysaetos* in England in 1986', *Ibis 130*: 564-565 (1988).

Warner, P. and P. O'Sullivan, 'The food of the pine marten *Martes martes* in Co. Clare', *Trans. Intern. Congr. Game. Biol. 14*: 323-330 (1982).

Whitaker, P., *Ferrets and Ferreting* (Pugs & Drummers, Dorset).

Xue-Liang, D., 'Labelling marmota himalayana with 32p for studying flea dispersal', *Acta. Entomologica. Sinica 26*: 179-184 (in Chinese) (1983).

Zielinski, W. J., 'Plague in pine martens and the fleas associated with its occurrence', *Great Basin Naturalist 44*: 170-175 (1984).

Index

Adele Island 43
Africa 16, 23
Aggression 89
Anal scent glands 12, 31, 89
Anglesey 33
Apples 39, 40, 74
Arran 33
Asia 16, 23, 32, 41 (*see also* South-
    East Asia)
Azores 33

Back/belly lines 26, 28
Baculum (os penis) 38 57, 91
Badgers 11, 46, 67, 72
Bats 103
Berries 39, 40
Birds (*see also* Seabirds, Native birds
    and Gamebirds)
    as prey 18, 19, 39, 40, 61, 77, 87
    as predators 16, 20, 21, 34
    eggs 88
    remains 91
    tables 98
    nests 67, 68
Black-footed ferret 55, 104, 106–7
Black-headed gull 75
Brains 87
Breeding 55–8
British Columbia 28
British Museum (N.H.) 7
Bute 33
Buzzard 34, 38

Cacheing 87–8
California 82
Camouflage 28
Canada 28, 45–6, 65
Canines 12, 88
Cannibalism 60
Captain Lyon 99

Captive small mustelids 56, 60, 98–
    100
    breeding 60, 105
Carrion 72
Cats 77, 106
Charm 23
Chicago Zoo 77
Children's stories 101–2
Chimpanzees 62
China 82
Chin-glands 82
Cine 61
Coat colour 25–30
Columbia 105
Competition 45
Conservation 103–7
Copulation 55
Crows 16

Dancing 22
Death 16
Deer 104 (*see also* Reindeer)
Delayed implantation 55
Dens 34, 42, 67–70, 80
    maternal/breeding 59, 67, 69
    sleeping 67
    temporary or bolt holes 67
Diet 71–4
Dispersing 63, 64–6
Distemper 107
Distribution:
    of weasel 16, 18
    of stoat 22–4
    of polecat/ferret 32–3
    of marten 38–9
Drabble, Phil 99, 111
Droppings (*see* Scats)

Ecological strategies 53–4
Ecologists 26, 45, 54

Energetics 54, 96–7
England 7, 19, 27, 38, 79
Erlinge, Sam 7, 11
Erlinge-Moors hypothesis 54
Ermine (see Stoat)
Extinction 104, 106

**Fauna and Flora Preservation
    Society** 109
Farmers:
    fur 12
    pig 33
Ferret (see Polecat)
Field studies 91–5
Finland 44
Fish 22, 74
Fisher 38, 51, 53, 54, 89, 96
Fleas 9, 26, 69, 80–82
Folklore 101–2
Food (see Diet)
Footprints (see Signs)
Fota Estate 9, 25:
    Wildlife Park 25
Foulmart/Foulmarten 32
Foxes 40, 77, 88
Fright 22
Frogs 34, 72
Fruit 39, 72
Fungi 72
Fur 48–9

Gamebirds 49–51, 73
Gamekeepers/game preservation 34,
    49–51, 65, 66, 74, 91
Gibbit 49
Gin trap 50
Golden eagle 76, 77, 79
Gopher 68
Grouse 74
Growing up 59–63
Guard hairs 32
Guernsey 42

Habitats 41–3
Hair 32
Hampshire 7
Harriers 38
Harris (island) 33
Harris, Peter 99
Harris, Steve 93
Hedgehog 32, 40:
    fleas 69

Insecticides 106
Interactions 44–7
Iowa 67
Ireland 9, 16, 38, 65–6, 72, 101–2
    Co. Cork 9, 25
    Co. Clare 9, 39, 72
    Ulster 9
Islands 42–3
Islay 42
Isle of Man 16, 24, 66

Jersey 42
Jura 42

King, C.M. 7, 112
Kites 34, 38
Kits (young) 59–62
Kiwi 103

Laboratory studies 91
Lapland 44, 64, 73
Legal protection 49, 51, 105, 106
Library 91
Lice 80
Lizards 72
Llandrindod Wells 34
Lockie, J.D. 112
Loos-Frank, B. 80, 112

Mademoiselle de Laistre 99
Mammal Society 77, 109
Man 48–51
Maori 103

Marten 35–40
  American 36, 66, 70
  beech 36, 82
  bib 35, 36
  old names 'marterns' and
    'martins' 35
May, R.M. 113
McInerney, Michael 7, 113
Mice 14, 18, 32, 40, 41, 46
Michigan 96–7
Ministry of Agriculture 34
Minivers 65
Mink 32, 36, 46, 88
Mites 80
Moles 18, 34, 68
Montana 66
Moorland 41
Moors, P.J. 113
Mull 33
Museum 91
Mustelidae/Mustela 11
Myxomatosis 46, 72

National Ferret Welfare Society 109
Native birds 43
Nature Conservancy Council 100,
  109
Nematode *Skrjabingylus nasicola* 80
Nest boxes 18
New Zealand 7, 12, 16, 23, 24, 41,
  51, 65, 72, 80, 94, 103–4
North America 16, 42, 49, 52, 65–6
North American Indians 101–2
Nuts 39

Oregon 28
Otter 11, 47, 77
Owls 14, 19, 77
Oxford University 18

Packs 61
Parakeets 26

Parasites 9, 80–82
Partridge 73–4
Persecution 49
Pheasants 74
Plague 84
Play 61–2
Poisons 105–6
Polar bears 75
Polecat
  ecological strategy 53–4
  ferret 33, 55, 58, 66
  marbled 104
  steppe 32
Porcupines 52
Poultry 72
Powell, R.A. 7, 77, 113
Prairie dogs 106
Predators 60, 65, 76–9
Primates 62
Ptarmigan 33

Rabbit 15, 16, 22, 33, 34, 46, 48, 49,
  50, 64
Radio tracking 25, 34, 42, 83, 94–5,
  96, 98
Rat 15, 16, 26, 33, 41, 48, 49, 50, 62,
  64, 68, 75, 106
Recognizing individuals 16, 36
References 111–14
Reindeer 44
Reintroduction 51, 52, 105
River valleys 33, 42
Road casualties 65–6, 91, 105
Rosehips 39
Russia (*see* Soviet Union)

Sable 36, 48, 104
Sandwiches 72, 98
Sardinia 33
Scats 39, 83–5
Scent 44, 31, 76, 89, 90, 92
Scientific studies 91–5
Scotland 25, 27, 38, 72
Seabird 43

Sex ratio 63
Sexual dimorphism 53–4, 96
Sexual maladjustment 98
Shrews 18, 40, 80
Sicily 33
Signs 83–8
Skeleton 12
Skrjabingylus nasicola 80
Skull 12, 19
Snakes 72
South-East Asia 105
Soviet Union 36, 42
Squirrels 16, 36, 40, 52, 61, 68, 69, 70
Stoat 20–26
  denning 23
  ecological strategy 53–54
  ermine 24
  Irish stoat 21, 26, 28, 30, 51, 68,
    72, 89, 93
  on islands 42–3
  social organization 46–7
  surviving 42
Surplus killing 72, 73, 75
Sweden 7, 46
  Revinge 64
Sweetmart/Sweetmarten 32
Switzerland 7
  Jura Mountains 64, 65

Tail 21, 77, 101
  drag 86
Takahe 103–4
Tame small mustelids 98–100
Teasey (a tame weasel) 99
Territory 18, 44, 84
  intra-sexual territorality 44
Terschelling 43
Ticks 9, 86
  Ixodes hexagonus 80
Tits 19
Toads 34, 88
Towns (*see* Urban areas)
Tracks (*see* Signs)
Tractors 86

Trapping 26, 49, 65, 89, 92
  continental trap 92
  Longworth trap 92, 93
  New Zealand stoat trapping
    system 94
  wire traps 93

United States 7, 28, 67, 99
University College, Cork 7
Urban areas 36, 41

Vet 100
Villages 36
Voles 14, 18, 32, 46
  field voles 72
  water voles 21, 22

Wales 9, 34
Washington State 28
Water 41
Weasel 14–19:
  black striped weasel 105
  ecological strategy 53–4
  family 13
  least weasel 14, 18
  long tailed weasel 18
  pygmy weasel 65
  short-tailed weasel 18
  Siberian weasel 105
  susceptibility to cold 92
  territories 18
  water weasel 105
Wedding ring 14
Whales 61
Wildlife parks 26, 36
Wildlife service
  Ireland 7
  New Zealand 103
Winter 28
  whitening 24, 27
Worms 11, 15, 34, 40
Wrap-around technique 23, 61
Wytham Woods 18–19, 97

Zoo 36